Cell Groups and
House Churches

What History
Teaches Us

Cell Groups and House Churches
What History Teaches Us

Peter Bunton

House to House Publications
1924 West Main Street · Ephrata, PA 17522

Dedication

To my parents,
James and Gwendoline Bunton, with gratitude for their
unstinting love and support over a lifetime.

Acknowledgments

I should like to express my gratitude to a number of people for their assistance, in different ways, in the writing of this book:

to the Revd. Dr. Ron Davies, formerly of All Nations Christian College, Hertfordshire, England, for his invaluable comments, suggestions and encouragement as he supervised my postgraduate dissertation which formed the basis of this book;

to Larry Kreider for his constant encouragement in ministry and in writing;

to my wife, Ruth Ann as she has carried some extra burdens, so that I might be released to the task of study and writing. To her I am particularly indebted; she is indeed a wife "worth far more than rubies" (Proverbs 31:10b).

to the editorial team at *House to House Publications* for their help and input.

Lastly I acknowledge the Lord for His continuing love, protection and guidance: He alone is worthy of all praise.

Contents

Foreword

This book is a treasure. I have never seen another like it any-where describing how cell groups and house churches are not only grounded in the Word of God, but in church history throughout the generations. Peter Bunton skillfully shows how small groups appeared historically to help revive and renew the church and meet one of mankind's basic needs for intimate fellowship and belonging.

The scriptures tell us, "There is nothing new under the sun." Principles on small group ministry that we discover in our day may seem new to us, but they are really only the resurfacing of truth that has been experienced by men and women of God throughout church history. Believers who have gone on before us have again and again been passionate to experience the Lord and His church in simplistic forms.

In *Cell Groups and House Churches: What History Teaches Us* we can learn many lessons from their holy experiment to establish family-like units of small groups. Why should we make the same mistakes that our forefathers made? Let's learn from them.

The treasures found in this book apply to Christian leaders and to all believers who have received a call from the Lord to experience genuine New Testament Christianity. These truths apply to both cell churches and to the new emerging house churches springing up around the globe.

During the past twenty years, Peter Bunton and his wife, Ruth Ann, have had a call to experience genuine church life first-hand that has centered in small groups in homes, much like the early church. It has been a joy for my wife, LaVerne, and me to know them and to walk with them in this journey. Thank you, Peter, for all of your research and hard work to make this book become a reality to help thousands of us in the body of Christ who are desiring to experience genuine Christian community in small groups through cell groups and house churches.

I highly recommend this book to you. The Lord has continued to restore His church in preparation for the coming harvest so we can become the spotless bride He has ordained us to be. Peter takes volumes of church history and narrows them down into this exciting, readable book that will challenge you and press you ahead in the Lord and in His purposes.

Larry Kreider
International Director, DOVE Christian Fellowship International

Introduction

God is raising the issue of cell groups and house churches all over the world today. Many of the new churches that have been planted in recent years are cell churches or house churches, and many of the new apostolic movements brought into being in our time are cell-based movements. A cell church usually has a number of cell groups meeting in homes, with these groups coming together regularly for congregational worship and teaching. With "house church," the small group meeting in the home is actually an autonomous church with its own eldership. These house churches may decide to network and meet with others in their local area, but the house church is fully *church* in its own right.[1] Whatever terminology is employed and distinctives there might be, nonetheless churches of very different denominational backgrounds are sensing that the Lord is speaking about bringing family groups back into the church, about appropriate structures for relationship, care, multiplication and growth. Much is being written on this vital subject.

So why a book on cell groups in church history? In mentioning the subject, a common response is "were there any?" The underlying assumption is that cell groups of any kind were extinct between the first century and the twentieth.

What happened between the first century church, when the believers were committed to one another and gathered together in small spiritual family groups as described in Acts 2:42-47, and today's cell group and house church movements? Some recent cell church literature does refer to historical precedents for what is happening today but this is usually only to mention a few names (such as Spener in the seventeenth century) and to assert that they were forerunners of today's cell advocates.

In researching the issue of whether cell groups were revived in the intervening centuries, I have found that neither of the above approaches is satisfactory. There have indeed been many times in the history of the church where attempts have been made to place the body in smaller family units, for discipleship, outreach and ministry. Some were similar to how cell church is seen today; others were first steps along the way which, for various reasons, never fully achieved their full potential in renewal and revival.

This book examines a number of kinds of small groups begun over the centuries since the Reformation. We have, however, already encountered a problem of language. Cell group, house church, small group—what term should be employed to describe the groups in this book, especially as many of the groups studied correspond neither exactly to cell group or house church as known today but foreshadow them? In any case, during much of church history such groups went under a variety of names such as *conventicles, collegia, societies,* or *bands.* Perhaps for now we should not delay inordinately over terminology but simply realize that we are dealing with the phenomenon of the rediscovery of small family units within the church and be somewhat satisfied with the generic term "small group" to cover this phonomenon, a term which has classically been defined as:

> a more or less cohesive collection of individuals who relate to each other personally and at intervals in more or less patterned ways because they share certain beliefs, values, affections, motives, norms, and roles and have a common goal.[2]

This book's aim is to investigate small groups and cell group movements to provide a historical background for what is happening today. To my knowledge there is no book which covers this ground, with, of course, the exception of a good deal of material on Wesley and his use of various small groups such as classes and bands. It is my hope that this addition will fill that gap in our understanding of those who have felt led by God to establish a new dynamic in church life. It is also hoped that it will add to our rationale of cell church and house church today, to show us historically those things which have worked and those which were problematic, and also to determine the theology which provides the basis for the flourishing of cells. There are indeed lessons for the church and its mission today.

In attempting to write a book of history, I am aware that I could quickly find myself writing rather tedious lists of who started small groups where and when. Of course various historical data must be provided, but an attempt will be made only to mention a few pertinent examples in each movement. For further historical exempla, the reader will be referred to other literature.

A second difficulty in writing such a book is that the writer wishes to substantiate the facts and opinions contained in the text. To do so on all occasions, however, would require an excessive use of footnotes and references, inappropriate for an introductory work on this subject intended for the general reader; such will therefore be kept to a minimum. Those requiring more research background are referred to the bibliography and to my unpublished dissertation.

A third problem is that of scope. Two thousand years of church history would be a long period for investigation! I will, therefore, limit this book to the 250 years or so after the Reformation. This is not to claim that there were no examples to be studied prior to the Reformation, nor in the nineteenth century. The Irish monks in the centuries after the fall of Rome displayed an understanding of small group in their apostolic movements, believing that twelve was the correct number for small religious community and missionary work. Furthermore, they displayed aspects of theology and ecclesiology similar to many of the movements of groups subsequent to the Reformation: they believed in women's ministry and leadership and the need for confession to an intimate friend (rather than a priest). A further study of such and other movements might prove fruitful but is beyond the scope of this book.

It is my hope that for many of those thinking through the issues of cell church or house church today, this text will provide some encouragement that they are not alone and that there is indeed "a great cloud of witnesses" who have gone before in various attempts to restore the life of Jesus to His body.

Peter Bunton
Luton, England.
September 2001

"Remember the former things, those of long ago;
I am God, and there is no other;
I am God, and there is none like me.
I make known the end from the beginning,
from ancient times, what is still to come."
Isaiah 46:10

"The real business of tradition is not the securing of the past,
but the ensuring of a future.
Only when we know how the story has run to this point can we
responsibly decide how the plot might now unfold."
—Luke Timothy Johnson
Scripture and Discernment
(Nashville, TN: Abingdon Press)

CHAPTER ONE

The Reformation

Martin Luther's Reformation: Were Small Groups a Part of It?

Martin Luther (1483-1546), the great Reformer, has been cited by many, both today and in the history of the church, in attempts to legitimize cell groups. Our investigation into the use of such groups subsequent to the Reformation will, therefore, begin with this key figure in the history of the church.

Luther is well known for his attack on the doctrines and practices of the Roman Catholic church. His rediscovery of the central tenets of salvation by faith and the final authority of the Bible initiated a powerful reform movement in the church.

But were there elements in Luther's theology and understanding of church (ecclesiology) which paved the way for small groups? Did he actually write about them? Did he, in breaking with so much of church tradition, ever begin to initiate and form small groups as part of his reformation of the church? Did his teachings advocate small groups in the church? These are key questions.

Luther saw that the true church was not reflected in the institutional church

There are a number of points in Lutheran ecclesiology which could be perceived as allowing the use of cell groups. Luther believed that the true church was not necessarily the same as the visible institution of church. In other words, he thought that a gathering of the true believers within the institutional was needed.

Luther believed every believer could teach, comfort and hear confession

His theology, moreover, provided for the universal "priesthood," meaning that every believer was a priest, able to go directly to God without the need of mediation by a select person.

If all were priests, then all could perform priestly functions. A number of his writings state that all could hear confession, administer absolution and teach:

> [For all are able] most freely to hear the confession of secret sins, so that the sinner may make his sins known to whomever he will and seek pardon and comfort, that is, the word of Christ, by the mouth of his neighbour.[1]

> This means that I may go to my friend and say to him, "Dear friend, this is the trouble and the difficulty which I am having with sin" and he should be free to say to me, "your sins are forgiven, go in the peace of God." You should absolutely believe that your sins are forgiven as though Christ himself were your father confessor—as long as your friend does this in the name of God.[2]

> Scripture expressly tells us to "encourage the fainthearted (1 Thessalonians 5:14) and "a dimly burning wick should not be quenched" (Isaiah 42:3), but rather nurtured. ...Therefore the Spirit reminds and admonishes us everywhere that Christians have authorization from God himself to teach and console one another....You should listen to me when I comfort you. ...I on the other hand, should listen to and believe you. ...There is tremendous weight in the word of the brother.[3]

Effective cell groups or house churches today require mutual sharing, prayer, confession and teaching; none of these would be disallowed by Luther's theology. On theological grounds, therefore, there could be no objection to believers meeting privately for the study of Scripture, teaching, confession of sins, prayer and the like. If there were a constraint, it would be in the area of church order, namely how correct teaching and practice might be maintained when the pastor was not present.

Luther taught that families are little churches

Apart from the general theological background, others believe that there are specific references to cell groups in Luther's writings. We know, for example, that Luther believed in and modeled how a family should meet for devotions. He wrote of the responsibility of parents to ensure their families were little churches, and he intended his edition of the catechism to be used in the family unit. Luther also advocated home-preaching.[4]

While the above is true, does it mean that Luther supported the formation of cell groups, other than the family unit itself acting as a small church? All the examples given are of the family, not a gathering of other believers from within the parish congregation. His modeling and written material were for family instruction. Furthermore, the examples of home preaching were of Luther himself, an ordained pastor. To deduce that he wished others to meet and instruct is conjecture, especially in view of his position that only some are called to minister in certain areas of the life of the church, a rather restrictive idea.

A strong case for small groups exists in Luther's *Preface to the German Mass*

Notwithstanding the above, Luther did on occasion specifically address the issue of the gathering of believers in small groups apart from the congregation. In his Good Friday Sermon of 1523, for example, Luther enunciated:

> One could gather separately those who believe correctly....I have been wanting for a long time to do it, but it has not been possible; for there has not yet been sufficient preaching and writing.

These sentiments were reiterated in his Easter Monday sermon a few days later: they expressed some desire to gather the true believers for edification. Of more importance, however, is the *Preface to the German Mass* of 1526. The following extract sets out his thinking on the kinds of worship structures that he wished to see. It is given at such length because in the subsequent centuries, a number would refer to it to claim justification for their own small groups:

> Now there are three different kinds of Divine Service.
> [1] The first, in Latin; which we published lately, called the

Formula Missae. This I do not want to have set aside or changed; but, as we have hitherto kept it, so should we be still free to use it where and when we please, or as occasion requires. I do not want in anywise to let the Latin tongue disappear out of Divine Service; for I am so deeply concerned for the young. If it lay in my power, and the Greek and Hebrew tongues were as familiar to us as the Latin, and possessed as great a store of fine music and song as the Latin does, Mass should be held and there should be singing and reading, on alternate Sundays in all four languages—German, Latin, Greek and Hebrew. I am by no means of one mind with those who set all their store by one language, and despise all others; for I would gladly raise up a generation able to be of use to Christ in foreign lands and to talk with their people, so that we might not be like the Waldenses in Bohemia whose faith is so involved in the toils of their own language that they can talk intelligibly and plainly with no one unless he first learn their language. That was not the way of the Holy Ghost in the beginning. He did not wait till all the world should come to Jerusalem, and learn Hebrew. But He endowed the office of the ministry with all manner of tongues, so that the Apostles could speak to the people wherever they went. I should prefer to follow this example; and it is right also that the youth should be practised in many languages. Who knows how God will make use of them in years to come? It is for this end also that schools are established.

[2] Next, there is the German Mass and Divine Service, of which we are now treating. This ought to be set up for the sake of the simple laymen. Both these kinds of Service then we must have held and publicly celebrated in church for the people in general. They are not yet believers or Christians. But the greater part stand there and gape, simply to see something new: and it is just as if we held Divine Service in an open square or field amongst Turks or heathen. So far it is no question yet of a regularly fixed assembly wherein to train Christians according to the Gospel: but rather of a public allurement to faith and Christianity.

[3] But the third sort [of Divine Service], which the true type of Evangelical Order should embrace, must not be celebrated so publicly in the square amongst all and sundry. Those, however, who are desirous of being Christians in earnest, and are ready to profess the Gospel with hand and mouth, should register their names and assemble by themselves in some house to pray, to read, to baptize and to receive the sacrament and practise other Christian works. In this Order, those whose conduct was not such as befits Christians could be recognized, reproved, reformed, rejected, or excommunicated, according to the rule of Christ in Matt. xviii. Here, too, a general giving of alms could be imposed on Christians, to be willingly given and divided among the poor, after the example of St. Paul in 2 Cor. ix. Here there would not be need of much fine singing. Here we could have baptism and the sacrament in short and simple fashion: and direct everything towards the Word and prayer and love. Here we should have a good short Catechism about the Creed, the Ten Commandments, and the Lord's Prayer. In one word, if we only had people who longed to be Christians in earnest, Form and Order would soon shape itself. But I cannot and would not order or arrange such a community or congregation at present. I have not the requisite persons for it, nor do I see many who are urgent for it. But should it come to pass that I must do it, and that such pressure is put upon me as that I find myself unable with a good conscience to leave it undone, then I will gladly do my part to secure it, and will help it on as best I can. In the meantime, I would abide by the two Orders aforesaid; and publicly among the people aid in the promotion of such Divine Service, besides preaching, as shall exercise the youth and call and incite others to faith, until those Christians who are most thoroughly in earnest shall discover each other and cleave together; to the end that there be no faction-forming, such as might ensue if I were to settle everything out of my own head. For we Germans are a wild, rude, tempestuous people; with whom one must not lightly make experiment in anything new, unless there be most urgent need.

Well, then: in the name of God. The first requisite in the German system of Divine Worship is a good, plain, simple, and substantial Catechism. A Catechism is a form of instruction by which heathen, desirous of becoming Christians, are taught and shown what they are to believe, to do, to leave undone and to know in Christianity. Hence mere learners who were admitted to such instruction, and were acquiring the rudiments of the Christian faith before their baptism were called catechumens. This instruction or information I know no better way of putting than that in which it has been put from the beginning of Christianity...[5]

Luther states that there are three different kinds of Divine Service: the Latin liturgy (*Formula Missae*), which he still wished to retain, principally because he wished young people to speak other languages; the mass in German, which he admitted was for the general population who were not "true believers or Christians;" and a third kind, the "true type of evangelical order" for those who are "desirous of being Christians in earnest." These groups were to meet in homes to pray, read, celebrate the sacraments, exercise discipline and minister to the poor.

The *Preface to the German Mass* legitimizes home cell groups
A number of pertinent points are raised in this text. Firstly, Luther is advocating some form of "believers' meeting," a meeting of the true church from within the visible church (in effect an *ecclesiola in ecclesia*, "little church within the church").

Secondly, we see the recommendation of some form of covenant between believers (the writing of names as a commitment).

Thirdly, it should be noted that such meetings were to be in homes.

Fourthly, one of the chief purposes for the groups was accountability and church discipline. The very reference to Matthew 18 indicates some belief in two or three gathering as actually being the church.

Fifthly, these groups should lead to some form of outreach or ministry.

It is entirely possible to see how later movements could appeal to Luther and this text for legitimization of their small groups meeting within the context of a larger congregation (the *ecclesiolae in ecclesia* concept), or even the notion of the believers' church, as many have, in fact, done. Luther's *Preface to the German Mass* was the basis on which others would build in the future.

Conclusion: Luther's writings encouraged but his actions discouraged the implementation of small groups

Those searching for Lutheran justification for the cells, however, often overlook the fact that Luther never implemented them (despite living some twenty years subsequent to writing the *Preface*). He claimed that people were not ready and that he did not have the co-laborers to bring this desire about, both of which were true to a degree.

When Luther did have people of a like mind, such as the reformer Lambert of Avignon who wished to implement this third order in Hesse by proposing voluntary groups within the state church, to meet weekly, be subject to discipline and desiring to evangelize those not part of the groups, Luther discouraged him from so doing for fear that the pastoral care of those outside the groups would be neglected. Although willing to shake the very foundation of the church on so many issues, he refused to do so on this one.

It is hard to imagine Luther being hindered from implementing a plan of *ecclesiolae* had he certainly wanted to do so. His concern for what the "tempestuous" Germans might do with it indicates his reason. His chief concern seems to be order, both church and state, for Luther needed to rely heavily on the civil authorities for his reformation. He also looked aghast at the direction in which the Radical Reformation was going. Thus, while glimpsing the possibility of a new kind of church renewal, Luther balked: there were to be no small groups.

It may be also that for Luther, they were a passing thought to be employed if a whole area did not wholly respond to his reformation and there might have been a need to convene at least some true believers. He wrote on 29 March 1527 that "the segregation of the true believers was to be effected within the parishes, *at least when the parishes were not prepared to go over as whole to the true Church*" (my italics). Luther was far more interested in reforming the majority church of a region than establishing small groups within it.

The Radical Reformation:
A Spontaneous Movement of Small Groups

The Radical Reformation began as a spontaneous movement of small groups, although it did not provide for them specifically in its developing ecclesiology or practice. Nonetheless, the ecclesiology which did develop, namely that of the "believers' church," was an influence on later cell group movements.

Believers' church

The believers' church concept stresses that the true church consists only of those who believed and who freely joined, as opposed to the concept of the state church or *corpus Christianum*, where all within a given territory are deemed to be Christians and church members. The Radical Reformation stressed discipline, that all were ministers and priests (the universal priesthood) and primitivism, the desire to return to the New Testament church in its belief, practice and structures. They wanted the church to return to the way it was in the first century, before it was corrupted by the Constantinian decree to establish Christianity as the religion of state in 324AD. In the Radical Reformation, this strong motivation to be the true church is shown by one of its leaders, Georg Witzel (1501-1573), who said:

> Which is the true [church]? the ancient apostolic. My wish, my yearning is that the world may go back to a true apostolic church. The Acts and the writings of the Great father and ancient bishops show the way on which we must go back to it. The apostolic church flourished to the time of Constantine. From then on it was perverted, because the Bishops went over to the world...[6]

These themes of wanting to be the true New Testament church in belief, practice and structure will appear among later seventeenth and eighteenth century groups, even by those denying the believer's church ecclesiology.

The burgeoning network of small groups had initially been encouraged by Zwingli and began in 1520. In the next three years, there was a wave of small group meetings in the Allied District of Zurich. These groups were often spontaneous rather than initiated by leadership as the following testimony concerning Andreas Castelberger (also known as "Andreas on the Crutches") shows. He taught in groups in Zurich beginning in 1522 until his banishment for so doing in 1525:[7]

> Heine Aberli, baker testified: Now that by the grace of God evangelical doctrine is being preached here in the city and elsewhere, —this witness—likewise [Lorenz] Hochrütiner of St. Gallen, Wolf [Ininger], cabinetmaker, and Bartlime [Pur], the baker, had at first with good friendly intentions planned to-

gether and reached a decision to meet and perhaps to choose and obtain someone who could open up to them the evangelical Christian teaching and the epistles of Paul and instruct [them]. Then they had gone into the home of this witness and begged Andreas on the Crutches that he undertake to do this with them as stated above, and teach them as well and as faithfully as he know and was able. But when they had met in his house for some time several good fellows contacted them on the street and asked if they could not also go with them and listen to the teaching that they were conducting among themselves. Then, when he and the others gave them permission insofar as it was done with good intentions, and their room was too small for them and not large enough, they had moved the teaching into the house of Herr Wolfgang, the chaplain, at his suggestion, meeting there several days. And now during these days there were so many of them that they needed still more space, and they went into the home of Hans of Wyl on his suggestion, and there Andreas on the Crutches gave them some good teaching. namely, reading, expositing, and explaining Paul's epistle to the Romans.

Small groups helped spread the Anabaptist message

In particular many of these groups began to study issues concerning the role of civil authority and the practice of baptism in the Scriptures. Because of their threat to the theology of the newly reformed church as well as the threat to the civil authorities, the city council of Zurich banned small group meetings on January 18,1525. On January 21, a group of about twelve men met once again in defiance of the ban and (re)baptized each other. This is usually taken as the starting date of Anabaptism.

Subsequent to the birth of Anabaptism, small groups continued, particularly as a means of spreading the Anabaptist message. The Nikolsburger Articles of 1527 state that, "The gospel is not to be preached openly in churches, but only in secret byways and privately in houses." [8]

Small groups were part of early Anabaptism missionary strategy. They had also produced the leaders of Anabaptism, many of whom had been trained in biblical interpretation and self-expression in the house meetings before the ban of 1525. These small groups were not *ecclesiolae* within the church of the masses; they were the beginnings of a movement of churches built on the ecclesiology of the believers'church.

The use of small groups in the Radical Reformation was expedient rather than out of a conviction of their necessity

The question remains to be asked, however, whether the Anabaptists were committed to the use of small groups in themselves, as an inherent part of the ecclesiology, or whether they were merely expedient. They were a new movement, small in numbers; due to persecution larger gatherings were difficult.

The concept of believers' church was in itself a limiting factor to size. Certainly the desire for the gathering of local believers in a (larger) congregation was the goal; ecclesiology was at the congregational level rather than the cell group level. It seems likely, therefore, that the use of small groups in early Anabaptism was expedient rather than out of conviction of their necessity.

The same applies to what might be described as the mainstream of the Radical Reformation. There were, of course, numerous other groups who come loosely under the categorization of Radical Reformation who also employed cell groups.

Some, such as Caspar Schwenckfeld of Silesia (1489-1561), were more mystical in tone. For him the true church was invisible and any attempt to organize it was futile, as truth was an inner quality. Small groups of like-minded souls could meet, however, for mutual edification. This was to be the only expression of church for such mystics.

Martin Bucer:
The Desire for True Christian Communities

A further key figure in the Reformation of the church in the sixteenth century was Martin Bucer (1491-1551) who spent most of his life in Strasbourg, in Alsace. Calvin was, in fact, Bucer's pupil.

On theological issues, Bucer stood somewhere between Luther and Zwingli, certainly on the doctrine of communion, or between the other reformers supporting the notion of majority church (that is, the church consists of all baptized in the locality) and that of the Anabaptists stressing the confessing or believers' church.

It is Bucer's ecclesiology and experiment with small groups which is of interest. Bucer believed the church to be where the Word was purely preached, willingly heard and where people were subject to Christ; this would be evidenced by the fruits of the Holy Spirit. He believed, moreover, that it was not possible ever to see the true church; the latter was certainly not the visible church consisting of all those baptized in a given area. He recognized that this outer church (the actual church) collected both the good and the bad within it.

The true church, however, was those led by the Spirit; it should be community, a community which the Spirit wished to bring into being. As early as 1523, he gave thought to such questions in his treatise, *That a Man Ought Not to Live for Himself, but for his Neighbour—And How He can Reach the Ideal.*

His position, however, was not that of the Anabaptists, who held to the notion of the believers' church. It was, in essence, a kind of synthesis between two different concepts of church, namely the majority church and the confessing church; it seems he wanted both combined. This may be similar to the desire we have already seen in Luther to have a majority state church, yet to call together the true, earnest Christians into small groups within it.

In terms of the subject of this book it is worth making the following observations. Firstly, for Bucer the church was something of the Spirit and to be brought about by Him.

Secondly, it was also to be communitarian; in his preaching and writings Bucer often stressed the passages in Acts, chapters two and four, as well as Romans 12 and 1 Corinthians 12.

Thirdly, the church was to follow the forms and practices of the early church, to which he strongly desired a return (primitivism). This kind of church community was "wahre christliche Gemeinschaft" (true Christian community).

Fourthly, it is worth noting that Bucer also believed that sanctification was a process and that the religious life was in developmental stages; people, therefore, needed assistance in progression through those stages of sanctification. This belief will be shown to be common in many key figures studied in this book.

Fifthly, discipline had a role to play in the purifying of the church; it was this which had been so sorely lost during history. As early as 1530, Bucer was writing, in *Enarrationes in sacra quattuor evangelia* that the text of Matthew 18:15-20 implied that small communities should be created on the basis of discipline.

The desire to return to the New Testament in both doctrine and pattern

By the mid 1540's, after some twenty years of his attempts to reform the church by teaching, writing, establishing various church ordinances as well as disciplinary procedures, Bucer was very disappointed with the church and the morals of many within it. He lamented the deficiencies of the Strasbourg church because he saw her defective apostolicity, that is that the church was not being faithful to the New Testament pattern. It was not a question merely of returning to the doctrine of the New Testament but also to its patterns and forms of community—it is the latter which would show the contemporary church to have apostolic faithfulness.

Due to the state of the church, coupled with the resurgence of Anabaptism in Alsace, Bucer became increasingly despondent, longing for a real example of church in Strasbourg. Matters were brought to a head in 1546 when the Protestant states including Strasbourg were defeated in the Schmalkaldic War, something which Bucer viewed as God's judgment upon their not having sufficiently reformed the church.

Bucer advocated a "second reformation" to begin in cell groups

Now was the time to act, in Bucer's mind, to be even more zealous and radical in church reformation. The following actions of Bucer have been described as an attempt at a "second reformation," [9] a phrase interestingly used in some cell church literature today for the restoring of cell groups to the church. [10]

This "second reformation" was to begin small groups, called "christliche Gemeinschaften" (Christian communities), which began early in 1547. The first written reference to them is found in the minutes of the Strasbourg town council of 21 February 1547:

> The preachers of St. Thomas and Young St. Peter's are convening the people in special meetings and assuming the right of excommunication. [11]

Hereafter Bucer wrote, in quick succession, a number of treatises on "Gemeinschaften," a pertinent example being *On the Need and Failure of the Churches and how to Improve Them* which showed

Bucer's strong primitivism. None was published in his lifetime nor for many years after his death (although we shall see that Spener discovered and published one such treatise, *On the increase of godly grace and spirit,* at the end of the seventeenth century).

What exactly was Bucer advocating?

In essence, Bucer proposed a two-phased plan. Firstly, the pastors were to preach on the need to be a true Christian community. Those interested would then receive a home visit from the minister who, if satisfied, would then invite them to a meeting. At the first meeting, the pastor again defined Christian community; one or two lay representatives were chosen to join the pastor and *Kirchenpfleger* (church trustee or guardian) to form a kind of leadership team. The pastor was to commit himself to serve the people and they him. Each person then received a private interview by one of the leadership team to ascertain their doctrine and state of repentance. If all was in order, they were registered as a member of the *Gemeinschaft* or community.

Bucer saw these groups as the means of bringing "the church to rest and unity." They were for aiding growth into holiness, both personal and in the whole parish. Within the communities there was open, honest fellowship, confession of sin (Bucer believed that corporate confession in public worship was not sufficient), accountability, including granting others permission to address issues seen in the member's life. There was also, to some degree, a sharing of goods and mutual practical provision for one another. Discipline was also exercised, ultimately in excommunication.

Such groups were Bucer's attempt to restore primitive Christianity; the early church provided the example for them, as one of his treatises states: *wie dan von der ersten kürchen vns das vorbild ist fürgestellet* (as the model is provided for us by the first churches). [12] Indeed he taught that partaking in such little communities modeled on the New Testament was the only way to keep the Ten Commandments.

Additionally, what is of interest is that each group remained connected to others. The leaders were to meet each week, and every one to two months there should be a meeting of all groups in the parish for teaching. (This has some semblance of the structure that Wesley was to establish some two hundred years later!)

Bucer was much criticized, for practicing excommunications and for what others believed was the implication that there were two classes of Christians, those in the parish and those in the communities. In defense, Bucer stated that the groups believed in the whole doctrine of the church and that they were trying to promote unity around these doctrines. He even stated that such groups were to be found in all evangelical churches, which they were not, and also in those churches that maintain Luther's order, which was also not the case.

Perhaps the critical issue, however, was that the civil authorities believed that the *Gemeinschaften* gave power of discipline and punishment to the church not the state; if the latter were to exercise its magisterial discipline properly then the *Gemeinschaften* were unnecessary. In November 1547, Bucer yielded somewhat and gave the civil authorities greater power over the *Gemeinschaften*. This, however, did not satisfy his opponents, and in January 1548, the *christliche Gemeinschaften* were banned. Officially they ceased to exist, although in effect they continued in the form of one large group for each parish.

In April 1548, Bucer visited England to return there in 1549 to live and teach at Cambridge University until his death in 1551. In England, he neither sought to establish small communities nor wrote further on them. Without his leadership or any other strong visionary advocate and under intense criticism including from many pastors, the Strasbourg communities completely ceased to exist in 1549. Perhaps one of the most notable fruits, however, was the influence Bucer's writings had on Spener (see Chapter Four) in the latter part of the seventeenth century, or certainly the justification for small groups which Spener was able to draw from them.

CHAPTER TWO

Conventicles—
The Puritan
Vision for Small Groups

In this chapter, we will look briefly at the use of small groups by the Puritans. Puritanism and Pietism have much in common; continental Pietism heavily influenced Puritanism. Puritanism, however, is so generally regarded as an English (including early colonial American) phenomenon that it will be treated separately in this survey of small groups as we move into the seventeenth century. Pietism will be discussed in the following chapter.

The initial Puritans were those dissatisfied with the form and life being developed within the Anglican church. They wished to stress greater "purity" (hence "Puritanism") in doctrine, ecclesiology and life. Emphasis was laid on depth of spiritual and devotional life and its outworking into the ethical and moral sphere.

These goals of a deeper life and rectitude in behavior were to be accomplished through a number of instruments. The personal devotional life was to be developed through reading of the Scriptures and other devotional works (of which the Puritans wrote many). In addition, great emphasis was placed on the continual preaching of the Word of God.

This led to practical application in life. Emphasis was given to observing the laws, how to behave in all manner of circumstances. Theology was to be outworked in reality. William Perkins, for example, one of the main figures in early Puritanism, wrote *A Golden Chain, or The Description of Theology, in Works of that Famous and Worthy*

Minister...Mr. William Perkins, (published in 1616) of which 31 pages were devoted to theology and 85 to practical concerns. This is indicative of Puritan values.

A good deal more emphasis was placed on intimate pastoral care of believers than in other traditions at that time. Private conferences were held with the minister or other experienced believer for guiding people to conversion and subsequent growth. This led some (and only some) to political action to purify their land.

As Puritanism developed in the seventeenth century, it changed from an appeal to the laws of God and logical deduction from Scripture to emphasizing the divine truth which the Spirit of God would impress upon a believer. Reason became somewhat subordinated to the authority of the Holy Spirit as intuitively discerned.

Conventicles develop to foster personal piety

With the regular Sunday service not lending itself to some of the chief aims of Puritans, such as practical application of the preaching heard, and with the necessity to be about one's devotional more often than Sundays, it should not be too surprising to see the development of various small group meetings within Puritanism (usually called "conventicles"). In 1596, John Udall in his *Certaine Sermons* wrote:

> After that the sermon is done, we ought at our coming home to meet together, and say one to another: "come, we have all been where we have heard God's word taught; let us confer about it, that we may not only call to rememberance [sic] those things that every one of us have carried away, but also that one may have the benefit of the labours of others." [1]

Puritan conventicles happened, however, not just on Sundays but in homes at other times, some weekly, others bi-weekly or monthly. John Eliot wrote that in them "we pray, and sing, and repeat sermons, and confer together about the things of God." [2]

Under the leadership of one minister at least, Cotton Mather (1663-1728), in New England, a veritable network of cell groups within his congregation was developed. Mather formed about 13 or 14 conventicles, each with around 12 members. They met in homes for prayer, Bible study, reading of sermons and devotional diaries. People were divided into groups according to gender and stage of life, as well as according to standing (e.g. tradesmen) and race (that is groups for white people and others for black people).

Conventicles change lives

That such conventicles were successful in their aims of transforming lives can be seen in the comments of Richard Baxter (1615-91) in his classic *Gildas Salvianus; the Reformed Pastor* (1656). He spoke of house meetings as bringing "more outward signs of success with most that do come than from all my public preaching to them." [3] Some one hundred years later, John Wesley was to make a similar observation.

Among the Puritans, therefore, conventicles did much in fostering personal piety and the moral and ethical outworking of faith. Puritan conventicles were not, however, seen as gatherings of the true church within the larger church, *ecclesiolae in ecclesia*, but were more akin to Anglican societies of which we shall read later, aimed at reforming behavior and regulating society. They also at times blended well with Puritan practice of "owning the covenant," whereby adults owned or renewed that covenant made on their behalf at baptism by their parents. This could lead to the establishment of various conventicles, as Samuel Danforth of Taunton, Massachusetts wrote in 1705:

> [The Covenant] was read to the brethren & sister in the forenoon, they standing up as an outward sign of their inward consent to the rest of the inhabitants....We give liberty to all men & women kind, from sixteen years old & upwards to act with us: & had three hundred names given to list under Christ against the sins of the times. The whole acted with such gravity & tears of good affection, as would affect an heart of stone....Its almost incredible how many visit me with discoveries of the extreme distress of mind they are in about their spiritual condition. And the young men instead of their merry meetings are now forming themselves into regular meetings for prayer [and] repetition of sermons. [4]

Quakers met in homes for prayer and Bible Study

Finally, some mention should be made of those Puritans who became disenchanted with mainstream Puritanism, especially the Quakers. This latter group wished to see the restoration of primitive Christianity and felt that church buildings, offices, liturgy, and sacraments were not part of that Christianity.

While still attending official places of worship they began to meet in homes for prayer and Bible study. They, through their leader, George Fox (1624-1691), began by calling the church to renewal but later came to see the movement as independent. It is noteworthy, however, that this fledgling, and ultimately unsuccessful attempt at ecclesiastical renewal should be through a network of small groups.

CHAPTER THREE

Pietism in the Reformed Churches

Pietism—A Reformation of Doctrine and Life

Pietism was a loose renewal movement within the Protestant church (and occasionally affecting some within the Roman Catholic church), from approximately the first half of the seventeenth century until the end of the eighteenth. Subsequent to Luther, the Reformation churches had stressed the need for doctrinal orthodoxy as the priority. The Pietists, while wishing to stand on the doctrinal truths of the Reformation, believed that following Christ was more than mere intellectual assent to orthodoxy. They stressed the need for a living relationship with God and for this to overflow in the fruit of good works. A definition of Pietism has been given as follows:

> Piety is the congruence in life of what is professed and what is practised; it is the congruence of faith and the fruits of the experiential reality known here as the fear of God, in which the believer seeks in no way to presume on God's grace but does everything possible to be an embodiment of truth and godliness. [1]

Perhaps the defining works of Pietist spirituality came from Johann Arndt (1555-1621) who wrote works such as *True Christianity* (1606) and *A Paradise Garden Full of Christian Virtue* (1616). In the latter we read:

> Ah, give me grace that I may help relieve and not make greater my neighbor's affliction and misfortune, that I may comfort him in his sorrow and all who are of a grieved spirit, may

have mercy on strangers, on widows and orphans, that I readily help and love, not with tongue, but in deed and truth. The sinner says the wise man ignores his neighbor, but blessed is he who has mercy on the unfortunate.

Pietism stressed conversion and a personal relationship with God as a gracious gift from Him, a transformed life shown by the fruit of good works, a belief in the Bible as the Word of God which was not only for doctrine but to effect everyday life.

To the Pietist, the study of Scripture became important in the pursuit of godliness. They, in fact, saw themselves as completing the Reformation, which to them had largely been a *reformatio doctrinae* but not a *reformatio vitae* (a reformation of doctrine rather than a reformation of life). For this to happen, there needed to be direct application of biblical insights to everyday life involving the laity's using the Scriptures for themselves.

Pietism was not a church or denomination but a term employed for those in all churches (Lutheran, Reformed, Separatist) with common spirituality. The centrality of *Wiedergeburt* (new birth) led to a loose fellowship of like-minded, reborn believers which has been called "a fellowship which crossed national and denominational borders and therefore made pietism the first ecumenical movement within Protestantism." [2]

Small groups, called *collegia*, are established to promote holiness and good works

Why should this movement concern us in a book on the history of the beginnings of cell groups in the church? Because as this renewal movement gathered pace, a common phenomenon was the establishment of small groups, usually called *collegia* or *collegia pietatis* (groups of piety), to study the Scriptures and promote holiness and good works. Such groups sprang up in the Reformed churches in Holland and German states (it would be anachronistic to use the term "Germany" at this period as there were many states comprising the area known as Germany today), in German and other Lutheran churches and in various radical or independent groups. They were, for many, a radical departure from the received understanding of church.

The Reformed Churches in Holland

A number within the Reformed Church in Holland were of the Pietist persuasion and began to form small groups. Among them was Jadocus van Lodensteyn (1620-1677) who stressed the need for reformation of the life of the church, holding small meetings for mature Christians and students which were devoted to experiential Christianity rather than theological disputes. For him, reformation of life should also include a concern of unbelievers.

William A. Saldenus (1627-1694) provided a theological basis for conventicles in his *De wech des levens* (first published 1667) by emphasizing the need to love the brethren (that is fellow Pietists) and to meet with them, while leaving others to the preachers.

Jean de Labadie (1610-1674), a Frenchman and former Jesuit living in Holland, established conventicles to help people separate themselves from the world as much as possible and to seek mystical union with God. These conventicles, held twice daily, both morning and evening, were to be the instrument for reformation within the Reformed communion. Labadie attempted to popularize conventicles in his writings. He even wrote in his book, *La réformation de L'Eglise par le pastorate (The Reformation of the Church by the Pastorate*, 1667), that establishing small groups should be one of the main occupations of the pastor. His groups were for both men and women together, although only the men were permitted to speak.

Some of the church groups were in fact separatist, such as those following Verschuir (1680-1737) and van Hattem (1641-1706). For them conventicles were for the meeting of God's people, chosen from eternity, who knew of their status through experiencing God's redemptive activity (rather than just knowing it to be so rationally).

The purpose and content of Dutch *collegia*

Conventicles in Holland during this period tended to be held on Sunday afternoon or a weekday evening. They were presided over by the pastor, the content including singing, reading and discussion of Scripture, discussion of the sermon and prayer. They also existed for the fostering of *koinonia* (fellowship) as they believed the early church had experienced it. This provides some hint of primitivism, the desire to return to the early church, which was to play a large part in the forming of cell groups in many of the seventeenth and eighteenth centuries movements.

Collegia Thrive in the German Reformed Churches

One of the most influential figures within German Reformed circles in the seventeenth century was Theodor Untereyck (1635-1693). In 1665, he began conventicles in Mühlheim. On Sundays, he met with interested men, while his wife led a women's group every weekday from 11am-12 noon. She also led groups on Wednesdays and Saturdays for servant girls, while Untereyck held a group for children.

In the city of Bremen there is evidence of conventicles on a city-wide basis, until ministerial opposition in the city brought many to closure. Even so, some women's groups continued. However, there is evidence that many class meetings in these areas, especially around Mühlheim, continued into the 1840's (that is almost two hundred years!) when historians believe they became seedbeds for a revival.

Both church and state authorities encourage home groups!

What was the response of the church authorities to this explosion of small groups? Interestingly, in the case of the German Reformed Church, it was mainly favorable. The Synod of Cleve in 1674 instructed ministers to permit conventicles, allowing individuals to invite their immediate neighbors into their houses for the purpose of reading the Bible, singing, praying and repeating the morning sermon. A more widely attended meeting could only be held in the presence of the pastor, who retained authority over them all. The minutes of the Synod read:

> In fact, all private conventicles must be conducted in a way which will not hinder public worship or bring it into disrepute. Furthermore, ministers and consistories shall have freedom to forbid anything which in their particular circumstances is not helpful or is dangerous, though it is otherwise permitted. [3]

The influence of Pietism's small groups upon the German lands was such that, by 1687 even some civil authorities were advocating cell meetings. In that year the town council of Wesel decreed that "Almighty God is to be served not only public in the congregations of the church, but also privatum," that is, in small house groups!

CHAPTER FOUR

Pietism in German Lutheranism

The Flourishing of Small Groups

Perhaps the largest body of Pietists, and certainly its most influential thinkers, namely Arndt, Philip Jakob Spener (1635-1705) and August Herrmann Francke (1663-1727), were within the Lutheran church. As mentioned in Chapter One, there was an awareness that the Reformation began by Luther needed to be brought to completion. As Spener wrote:

> I have never been of the opinion and am not so now, that the reformation of Luther was brought to completion as one might hope. [1]

There was, furthermore, a widely held view that specifically in the establishment of *collegia* or cell groups that the Lutheran reformation was being completed in ecclesiastical structures. We have already investigated Luther's stance on the issue of small groups. What is important here, however, is the legitimacy which the Pietists believed his ecclesiology gave their effort. This was based upon three things; firstly, they believed Lutheran theology and ecclesiology paved the way for small groups because Luther allowed for the true church's not being coterminous with the visible institution, thereby allowing some kind of small group within the parish for true believers. His theology provided for the universal priesthood; all could hear confession, administer absolution and teach. Secondly, it could be asserted that Luther employed small groups, as was seen in Chapter One. Thirdly, and most pertinently, are the comments Luther made in the *Preface to the German Mass* of 1526 (see Chapter One).

Spener promotes an understanding of "church" which paves the way for small groups

Philip Jakob Spener is perhaps the most influential of all Pietists, largely due to his writings and his clear enunciation not just of doctrines but of a seminal program for church renewal.

There are four key points in Spener's thinking which form the background to his promotion of cell groups, namely "new birth" and subsequent sanctification, the use of Scripture, the nature of the church and of the spiritual priesthood.

In 1696, Spener wrote a series of sixty-six sermons on the subject of "new birth." For him this was central, not just as a one time experience but that it should work itself out in the process of growing in holiness (sanctification).

Secondly, the place and use of the Bible is important to an understanding of Spener; the Bible was infallible but it had to be illuminated by the Spirit and interpreted by the believer. He advocated to his Bible study groups, therefore, not a scholastic approach of word studies but the need to take Scripture in context and as a matter of prayer:

> No practice will prove more pleasant or beneficial, and none more suitable to the College [i.e. small group], than after fervent, secret prayer, to discriminate and enter into the Affections of the Inspired Writers with sacred attention and perseverance, and strive to unfold their nature and character.... When engaged in the study of the Scriptures, the idea formed in the Writer's mind should be carefully ascertained; the Affections by which he was influenced; his state of life; and his office at the time he penned the book.... Luther again remarks, "that an expositor should, as it were, invest himself with the Author's mind, in order that he may interpret him as another self." [2]

Thirdly, it is in the area of ecclesiology or understanding of the nature of church that Spener made his most far-reaching contribution. For Spener, the church existed where the Word of God was preached and the sacraments rightly administered (the orthodox Lutheran position). However, the outer form of that church was in abject condition and needed renewal. He drew a sharp distinction between the church as a building and the church as people:

[By church] one doesn't mean the building that is dedicated to the worship of God and is used for that purpose. Such churches of which we speak are "meeting houses." One understands by the word "church," however, the gatherings of Christians, in general as well as in certain special groups. The former is the universal; the latter are the singular churches. [3]

Furthermore there was a clear distinction between the inner church and outer church, the invisible and visible church, true believers and nominal Christians:

the righteous believers who have the true, divine living faith, and therefore find themselves not only in the outer assembly, and confess themselves to Christ, but who through such faith in him, cleave to the true head, and out of him, as the branches out of the vine, receive living sap and spirit, and bring forth fruit out of the same. Thus we can imagine the entire outer Christian church as a tree which has dry and green branches. [4]

Although accepting that there would always be the "wheat" and the "tares" growing together until the Day of Judgment he, nonetheless, wished to reform the church so that, as far as possible, the invisible and visible were coterminous. Spener saw the pre-Constantinian church as the ideal and goal. Here again, we see primitivism as a motivational force.

A further essential understanding relevant to the promotion of small groups is Spener's understanding of spiritual priesthood. He was clear that all Christians were priests and could exercise priestly ministry:

[spiritual priesthood is] the right which our Savior Jesus Christ purchased for all men, and for which He anoints all believers with His Holy Spirit, in the power of which they may and shall bring sacrifices acceptable to God, pray for themselves and others, and edify themselves and their neighbors. [5]

Christians, including women, have the power and right to meet together for these purposes (although women were not to teach in a public congregation). The *Spiritual Priesthood* explains to pastors how they should encourage *collegia pietatis* (small groups) for the ends mentioned above.

Spener Advocates and Establishes
Small Groups (*Collegia*)

Collegia began while Spener was a minister in Frankfurt in 1670. Having preached a sermon on the righteousness of the Pharisees, Spener was approached by a number of parishioners for further guidance on how to make the Bible the central guide to their lives, as he had been preaching in his sermon. Small study groups, independent of pastoral control, were proposed and initiated. Having discussed this matter subsequently with other pastors Spener made the decision to lead the groups himself in the hope of avoiding any possible separatist tendencies that might emerge.

The groups met on Mondays and Wednesdays. The Monday meeting usually reviewed the main points of the Sunday sermon, discussing how this could be applied to everyday life. At the Wednesday meetings, a portion of Scripture was explained and discussed, followed by prayer. The only "rule" for these groups was that everything should be edifying.

Spener's vision

Such meetings had already been on his mind as we see from his devotional writings of 1669:

> How much good it would do if good friends would come together on a Sunday and instead of getting out glasses, cards, or dice would take up a book and read from it for the edification of all or would review something from sermons that were heard! If they would speak with one another about the divine mysteries, and the one who received most from God would try to instruct his weaker brethren! If, should they be not quite able to find their way through, they would ask a preacher to clarify the matter! If this should happen, how much evil would be held in abeyance, and how the blessed Sunday would be sanctified for the great edification and marked benefit of all! It is certain, in any case, that we preachers cannot instruct the people from our pulpits as much as is needful unless other persons in the congregation, who by God's grace have a superior knowledge of Christianity, take the pains, by virtue of their universal Christian priesthood, to work with and under us to

correct and reform, as much in their neighbors as they are able according to the measure of their gifts and their simplicity. [6]

This shows that the universal priesthood was fundamental to his understanding of cell groups and that he recognizes that the work of God cannot be carried out alone by the ministers. It is also observable that preaching alone is not sufficient for renewal unless it is in some way applied—and that this is best done in small groups.

Tracing the key influences on Spener's *collegia*

It seems that the actual initiation and implementation of small groups in Frankfurt, however, should not actually be credited to Spener. This is a contrary view to much that has been written on this matter. Spener, in fact, never asserted that the founding was his idea. We know that four key members of the groups who approached Spener after his sermon were Johann Jakob Schütz, Johannes Anton Tieffenbach, Zacharias Conrad Uffenbach and Johann Christoph Uffenbach. It is possible, even likely, that these young men had been to Holland and seen *collegia* in existence there.

The key influence on them, however, was the writing of Jan Amos Comenius (1592-1670). Comenius had written comments on Luke 10:42 that the "one thing necessary" (*unum necessarium* in Latin) in life was to worship Jesus and devote oneself to him, just as Mary had done in this passage of Scripture. If believers followed this example, the world could be changed.

Comenius' work was published in Amsterdam in 1668 and was widespread in Frankfurt in 1670; in fact Schütz placed a copy in a library for others to read. When these four approached Spener in 1670, they actually stated that they wished to speak *de uno necessario* [7] (about one thing necessary), a phrase which Spener himself used in his program for church renewal, *Pia Desideria* in 1675. The central impetus in forming the groups, therefore, came not from Spener himself, but others, who were chiefly motivated to establish an environment where they could respond to Jesus as Mary had done in Luke 10.

It was this which led to the birthing of small groups in Frankfurt. Spener's role was to bring some element of order, direction and control, particularly as has feared any separatist tendencies after learning of de Labadie's separatist group which began in 1669.

Although perhaps not wishing to acknowledge this widely, it is likely that in this as well as his reliance on the passage of 1 Corinthians 14 for biblical justification for his work, Spener was influenced by de Labadie. Labadie, in his *La réformation de L'Eglise par le pastorate* (1667), which circulated in Frankfurt 1674-5, stressed the critical importance on the ecclesial model of 1 Corinthians 14. Spener also sought justification for *collegia pietatis* from Matthew 18, as both Luther and Bucer had done before him.

The need but failure to multiply

By the end of 1670, there were some 15 to 20 men attending the Frankfurt group. In the following year, Spener was thinking of multiplication and looking for suitable pastors to take some members and begin a second group. This did not materialize. In 1675 there remained but one group, with some 50 members. By this time, more unlearned men and also women (who nonetheless sat in another room from where they could hear but not be seen!), were attending.

Due to size, Spener relinquished the objective of intimate fellowship. There was a clear and discernible change of content to focusing on the study of the Scriptures: "We laid aside human books and took up the Holy Scriptures themselves with a childish simplicity." [8]

Spener: The apologist for small groups

Subsequently Spener developed more fully a program for church renewal, seen most clearly in his *Pia Desideria* of 1675. Snyder [1989] analyzes this program as having six main foundations: greater use of the Word of God, particularly in homes and contexts other than the sermon; the exercise of the spiritual priesthood; the essence of Christianity to be seen as love and good works; controversies were to be dealt with in gentleness and prayer; pastors should be trained in piety including through the medium of cell groups; sermons were to be directed to produce piety. Perhaps the best hope of church renewal was the recovery of the Word of God as the spiritual priesthood gathered, for Scripture study changed people; "The Word of God remains the seed from which all that is good in us must grow." [9] He later added that:

> ...it cannot be wrong if several good friends sometimes meet expressly to go over a sermon together and recall what they

heard, to read in the Scriptures, and to confer in the fear of the Lord how they may put into practice what they read. Only the gatherings should not be large, so as not to have the appearance of a separation and a public assembly. Nor should they, by reason of them, neglect the public worship or condemn it, or disdain the ordained ministers.[10]

Spener's groups were not to be separatist but an expression of the invisible church, firmly, however, within the visible: they were to be "little churches" within the larger church, namely *ecclesiolae in ecclesia.*

The desire to return to the New Testament church

Spener was motivated by primitivism, for he wanted to have cell groups in order "to reintroduce the ancient and apostolic kind of church meetings" based on 1 Corinthians 14:26-40:

For a third thing it would perhaps not be inexpedient (and I set this down for further and more mature reflection) to reintroduce the ancient and apostolic kind of church meetings. In addition to our customary services with preaching, other assemblies would also be held in the manner in which Paul describes them in 1 Corinthians 14:26-40. One person would not rise to preach (although this practice would be continued at other times), but others who have been blessed with gifts and knowledge would also speak and present their pious opinions on the proposed subject to the judgment of the rest, doing all this in such a was as to avoid disorder and strife.... Then all that has been contributed, insofar as it accords with the sense of the Holy Spirit in the Scriptures, should be carefully considered by the rest, especially by the ordained ministers, and applied to the edification of the whole meeting.[11]

Spener also wrote that he believed Jesus had taught in homes and that, on the basis of 1 Corinthians 16, the early church had also met in homes.

The outcome of Spener's attempt at renewal

It seems that a variety of people attended Spener's groups at some time: artisans, servants of both sexes and the social élite. It is interesting to note that as the numbers attending increased and, particularly because of criticism, Spener changed the location of meetings from homes to the church building; this was to some considerable detriment:

> in that some of the middle class who had often spoken something for their own and others' upbuilding in the home, ceased to speak in such a public place and thus a certain part of the previous fruitfulness was lost. [12]

It should also be noted that due to further opposition on the grounds that he was replacing the confessional, that he was too spiritualistic and undermining the leadership of the church, as well as a number of his friends leading their groups to separation from the Lutheran church, Spener eventually actually stopped all such *collegia*.

As late as 25 January 1701, however, he was writing "My principle has always been, and I do not diverge from it yet, to form *ecclesiolae in ecclesia*—for unity and closer fellowship." When he, in later life, ministered in Dresden and Berlin, however, he began no conventicles. The lack of effect on the institutional church and so many seeing the only way forward as separation were disappointments to him.

The Link Between Spener and Bucer

In 1691, Johann Schilter, a professor at Strasbourg and a friend of Spener's, found a copy of Bucer's *Mehrung götlicher gnaden und geists,* written in 1547 concerning his small communities. Schilter sent a copy to Spener who published it in 1691 and again the following year.

Some assert that Bucer was an influence on Spener in his founding of the *collegia*, but a closer inspection of the dates reveals that Spener, despite originating in Alsace, only learned of Bucer's attempt at small groups some twenty years after his own attempts began. Rather than Bucer's being an influence on Spener it would be more appropriate to assert that, having instigated a program for church renewal through small groups, when finding Bucer's writings, Spener was able to use them to justify his ecclesiology and practice.

Francke's Use of *Collegia*

At the university in Leipzig (1689-92) and then later at the city of Halle, August Herrmann Francke, a younger colleague of Spener's, began a small group which, at times, was attended by the very highest members of society, even by members of the imperial and royal families and their officials.

This group met weekly; members read, in turn, a portion of the Bible in Hebrew or Greek and commented thereon, seeking to find the literal meaning. Over time, the content turned to a more devotional nature. They began and ended with prayer. A Pietist source, the *Pietas Hallensis*, describes the meetings:

after the lecture, both explicatory and applicatory of the text, it was a custom for the director to add his admonitions and counsels, the rest of the members to confer their observations, and even the students and auditors sometimes to propose theirs too. [13]

Small Groups Proliferate and Become Widely Accepted

Numerous other Lutherans employed conventicles. Indeed a number predated Spener. Martin Moller (1547-1606) held conventicles among his congregation in Görlitz, as did Heyland in Butzbach in 1623. In Halberstadt, Ammersbach attempted to form a *Society of the Lovers of Jesus*, as had Ahasverus Fritsch.

In Essen, class meetings proliferated from the latter part of the seventeenth century onwards. In the 1670's even the mayor was holding conventicles. In 1702, between 60 and 150 people were attending Wednesday meetings and from 400 to 500 met in conventicles on Sundays. It was these meetings which formed the basis of the religious awakening that happened in the Duchy of Berg in 1727.

In Württemberg (currently in the southwestern part of Germany), conventicles particularly flourished. Spener, on his visit to Tübingen in Württemberg in 1662, led two *collegia*, one for university personnel and one for the nobility. In 1703, three tutors from the theological foundation associated with the University of Tübingen, S.C. Gmelin, J. Oechslin and J. Rebstock, gathered on Sunday afternoons in a wine dresser's hut outside the town to read and discuss the Bible, with a number of young people attending; this occasioned a small revival.

Others sprang up and became widely accepted during the eighteenth century. These meetings were called *Stunden* (hours): the majority were within the Lutheran church, led by the pastor or someone appointed by him, usually meeting on Sunday afternoons. A number did meet apart from the church, around someone recognized as a leader, while others separated from the church.

Conventicles inevitably drew the attention of the authorities in Württemberg. In 1703, they tried to contain the growth of conventicles by an Edict which seems to have little effect. Concern arose at different stages during the first half of the century (they were particularly concerned with conventicles in Stuttgart in 1710 because they met until midnight!).

In 1743, however, the civil authorities in Württemberg passed the General Rescript granting the right of private religious meetings to those qualified to hold them, that is lay people who were under the supervision of a pastor, as long as conventicles were not held during the hours set aside for regular worship in the church.

CHAPTER FIVE

Radical Pietism

Radical Pietist Conventicles

In addition to those Christians forming conventicles within the Lutheran and Reformed Churches, there were others who were independent of, or who separated from, the churches.

Mention has already been made of de Labadie. Eventually he became congregationalist and was suspended by the Reformed synods. He traveled to Amsterdam where he procured a large house, with a hall for meetings, and he began (1669) a separatist *huiskerk* (house church) to bring together in close fellowship those who were truly converted.

This was in effect a communitarian form of Pietism, still largely Reformed in theology. Indeed members traveled to encourage people to hold on to the Reformed faith but to separate themselves by establishing communities. It seems that their meetings were even characterized by the ecstatic.

Mystical Pietism

Around the same time, a *collegium* was founded by Giesbert and four Van der Kodde brothers. This grouping became known as the Collegiants, a loose term for an even looser joining of various individuals of an illuministic and mystical bent. They were largely Anabaptist in theology, encouraged free prophecy in their meetings, tried simply to maintain an ethic of love and to live according to the Sermon on the Mount. For them, small groups replaced the church; they doubted the very possibility of a visible church.

A whole stream of Pietism developed that was mystical in nature. Due to the stress on the personal inner relationship with God and the quest for union, many of these were extremely suspicious of church institutional arrangements. Some, such as Dippel (1673-1734), wrote of gathering the true church out from all existing sects.

In 1725-27, there was a revival and a concomitant circle of conventicles in Mühlheim under the quietist Wilhelm Hoffmann. Gerhard Tersteegen (1697-1769) was converted through them and in 1727 began establishing communities, especially in the Ruhr area. He did not wish to start a sect but did talk of "membership" of these groups. The orthodox in Mühlheim were, of course, alarmed at many of these groups. They succeeded in having all conventicles banned by law from 1740-1750. When allowed to do so again, Tersteegen began a conventicle in his home in 1750. Again this was of a more quietistic temperament.

Other groups sprang up who were more Anabaptist in theology, others inspirationist, some even practicing glossolalia. One such Anabaptist group, called the Dunkers, founded in Wittgenstein, was led by Alexander Mack (1679-1735). Mack gives an account of the small group meetings held in 1709:

> When they come together they sing two or three hymns, as God moves them; then they open the Bible and whatever they find they read and explain it according to the understanding given to them by God, for the edification of their brethren. After they have read, they fall to their knees, raise their hands to God and pray for the authorities, that God might move them to punish the evil and protect the good; then they praise God that he has created them for this purpose. [1]

Lastly, mention should be made of the Inspired movement of the early decades of the eighteenth century. They believed in the continuance of the prophetic gift, were separatistic and founded small groups for private and public proselytizing as they engaged in itinerant evangelism.Their self-definition was as an *ecclesia ambulatoria* or *Wanderkirche* (roving church). They were centred on the Wetterau around Mannheim, Heidelberg, Frankfurt, Cologne and Marburg but also established small groups in Swabia, Zweibrücken and also in Switzerland in Bern, Zurich and Schaffhausen, all in contact and fellowship with the congregation in Wetterau.

Small Groups Outside of Holland and Germany

Clearly it is impossible to record every known instance of believers meeting in small groups which might loosely fall under the Pietist banner. However, one or two other occurrences should be mentioned to show that the movement spread beyond Germany and Holland. In **Silesia**, due to opposition, Protestantism in the latter part of the seventeenth century was an underground, and lay-led movement, meeting in *collegia* along the Spenerian model. In 1707, the children of Glogau held their own outdoor meetings and revival broke out, which spread in 1708 to Breslau.

Around the same area of **Lower Silesia**, Johann Steinmetz (1689-1762) was preaching in the villages and winning many to Christ. He established cell meetings and prayer meetings, among which many visions took place. He also went to Polish-speaking Teschen where a revival broke out from children's camp-meetings. Such Silesian conventicles were in fact not *ecclesiolae in ecclesia* for they supplanted and replaced the meetings of the church.

In **Sweden**, Pietism was on the ascendancy in the 1720's with a number of conventicles in operation. These, however, were banned by law (*Konventikelplakat* of 1726), but some continued. In Amea, in the north of the country, Nils Grubb held gatherings in barns and on hills, while at Nordalming, Nils Jannson Ulander established conventicles for singing spiritual songs, gospel reading and extemporary preaching. Both these men saw large numbers converted.

Protestants in **Austria** were a small, persecuted minority. From 1683, many miners from Salzburg met together secretly in the woods. They prayed, sang and read Scripture, the catechism and other good books. These groups were an underground church. A revival spread to the extent that the authorities could no longer tolerate their meetings, and in 1731 some twenty thousand fled the country.

An Assessment of *Collegia Pietatis*

Pietist *collegia,* as we have seen, occurred in many different places over more than two centuries. They were usually either weekly or twice weekly meetings. Some were led by pastors, others by laity. Whatever the leadership, there was considerable lay participation. The emphasis was on personal holiness and edification, including study of the Scriptures but not in the dry scholastic way merely to understand doctrine.

Instead, they studied the Scriptures to raise faith, hope and love, primarily through the use of three chief questions when approaching the text:

"What does it teach?"

"What does it command?"

"What promise or hope is given?"

While perhaps not displaying such an emphasis on discipline as in Anabaptist churches or indeed as in later Wesleyan groups, there was, nevertheless, an aspect of confessional with them. Everyone was to seek a *geistlicher Vater* (spiritual father), a lay person to hear one's confession (usually the group leader).

Pietist *collegia* were successful in that they facilitated personal holiness in many (often leading to good works); they encouraged and developed ministries among the laity, including leadership; they also achieved a high degree of equality and unity among people from differing social backgrounds.

Their success too was due to having a well-reasoned ecclesiological basis and rationale, thanks largely to Spener, as well as a strategy for multiplication, where leaders were expected to initiate the founding of new groups (although as we have seen, Spener himself was not able to produce significant multiplication). Pietism's effects on church life and society were great: many pastors were Pietist, especially in the movement's heyday in the earlier part of the eighteenth century. Vast quantities of literature and educational materials were published, schools and social programs were developed, foreign missions were initiated.

The small groups fostered the holiness behind church life and social action. In Germany, it seems that the groups tended to do well in the more affluent cities, for example, Frankfurt, Hamburg and Dresden, rather than among the lower classes and rural areas (with the very notable exception of Swabia).

CHAPTER SIX

Anglican Religious Societies

A further interesting stirring by God led to a loose movement of small groups occurring in the latter decades of the seventeenth century in the Anglican church in England. The groups became known as *religious societies*. While being more formal than the Pietist groups (and a lot more regimented than we would have cell groups today!), the name *society* in some ways belies that fact that these were essentially small groups of people gathering to encourage one another in personal holiness and in works of compassion.

Horneck Establishes "Societies" to Promote Holiness

The first such society in England dates from the 1670's (approximately the same time as the beginnings of Spener's *collegia pietatis*). The widely recognized founder was Dr. Anthony Horneck (1641-1697), a German Lutheran, who came to England in 1661, turned Anglican and eventually became the preacher at the Savoy Chapel in London in 1671.

The contemporary *Account of the Rise and Progress of the Religious Societies in London* [1] describes the beginnings when several young men "were about the same time touched with a very affecting sense of their sins, and began to apply themselves in a very serious manner to religious thought and purpose." The account continues:

> it many times fell out...that several of them met together, at the house of their spiritual physician, seeking cure for their wounded spirits; and so contracted a little acquaintance by those providential interviews. [2]

Horneck and others advised them that they should meet once a week and "apply themselves to good discourse, and things wherein they might edify one another." The young men did so, soon finding:

> the benefit of their conferences one with another; by which, as some of them have told me with joy, they better discovered their own corruptions, the devil's temptations, and how to countermine his subtile devices; as to which, each person communicated his experiences to the rest.[sic] [3]

From this mutual encouragement to holiness issued a compassion for others and good works:

> the first design of those who joined in this religious fellowship looked no farther than the mutual assistance and consolation one of another in their Christian warfare. That by their interchanged counsels and exhortations, they might the better maintain their integrity in the midst of a crooked and perverse generation. But as their sense of the blessedness of religion, and the value of immortal souls, increased, they could not but exercise bowels of compassion towards such as discovered little concern about these important matters. [4]

Such societies numbered 40 in London alone in 1700, with, for example, a further nine or ten to be found in Dublin, comprising some three hundred people.

It is discernible that the primary aim of the societies was personal spiritual growth and holiness of life. Strict rules were drawn up by Horneck to reflect this of which the final rule seems to encapsulate the aim of the small groups to promote individual holiness:

> Rule XVIII. The following Rules are more especially to he commended to the Members of this Society, viz. To love one another: When reviled, not to revile again: To speak evil of no man: To wrong no man: To pray, if possible, seven times a day: To keep close to the Church of England: To transact all things peaceably and gently: To be helpful to each other: To use themselves to holy Thoughts in their coming in and going out: To examine themselves every night: To give every one their due: To obey Superiors both Spiritual and Temporal. [5]

The rules show that these groups were firmly within the Church of England, indeed led by an ordained minister, with devotions according to prescribed patterns. (Later, the necessity of the meeting being led by an ordained minister was relaxed.) A due was also paid which was, at stated times, redistributed to the poor.

The societies were initially for men, but women did join later. At a time when church discipline was non-existent, the societies provided perhaps the only disciplinary function within Anglicanism. Despite seeming formal and regimented, by modern standards, there was much freedom to share about their walk with God, struggles with temptation and sins and mutual prayer and exhortation to godliness. Although contained within strict boundaries, such groups were innovative and radical in their time.

The desire to restore the New Testament church

It is interesting to note that a prime motivation behind these small groups was the desire to return to the New Testament church (primitivism). A key work at this time was William Cave's (1637-1713) *Primitive Christianity: or, the Religion of the Ancient Christians In the first Ages of the Gospel* (1661), which stressed that primitive Christianity was the model to imitate in personal godliness and church life. Horneck also stressed that the societies should initiate a return to the early church:

> We are not to regulate our religion by the sickly Fancies of half Christians, but by the standing Laws of Jesus...whom the Primitive Believers thought themselves obliged to follow in external, as we as internal simplicity. [6]

He, along with others we have already encountered in this survey of historical figures promoting small groups, believed in the notion of a falling away of the church from its original state and intention, and he wished to see a restoration. Other contemporaries were even more explicit, such as William Whiston who in 1715 published *Proposals for erecting societies for Promoting Primitive Christianity.* [7]

The dual objectives of sanctification or perfection and early church restoration are aptly summarized by an anonymous contemporary biographer of Horneck who states that he strove to bring:

The best of his parishioners to a higher state of Christian perfection, to more pure and primitive lives than they practicesed [sic]. He always had in view the innocence and simplicity of the first professors of our most holy religion and burned with an ardent desire of bringing our practices to their standard. [8]

It is furthermore interesting to note that this biography also writes, as did Comenius and Spener, of the importance of the "one thing necessary" (*unum necessarium*) to obtain salvation.

A Key Book Influencing the Formation of Societies
A Country Parson's Advice to His Parishioners

An anonymous book with the above title was published in 1680 and had far-reaching influence, including on John Wesley. The book exhorted people to make a commitment to lead a holy life, containing a number of advices to facilitate its achievement. One of the means of achieving holiness was to find others who had made a similar vow. The committed should become "bosom friends" with such people and seek "their prayers, their instruction, their reproofs, their encouragements...." This seminal work continues:

> And let me tell you that if good men of this Church will thus show themselves, and unite together in the several parts of the country, disposing themselves into fraternities, or friendly societies, and engaging each other, in their several and respective combinations, it will be helpful to one another in all good Christian ways. It would also be the most effectual means for restoring our decaying Christianity to its primitive life and vigour, and the supporting of our tottering and sinking Church. [9]

Two Kinds of Society:
Religious societies
Societies for the Reformation of Manners

A closer analysis shows that two different kinds of societies existed in the late seventeenth and early eighteenth centuries in England. One was the religious society on the Horneck model, while the other was the society for the "Reformation of Manners." While it has been shown that the religious society was for developing personal piety as well as good works, the latter aimed more at societal reformation, usually by attempting to stop vice, to ensure that criminals were arrested, and to distribute upbuilding literature. Josiah Woodward, in his contemporary (1698) account of both types, made the following distinction:

> For though they all agree in the Promotion of Virtue, and Opposition of Vice, yet their first and more direct Design of Association seems to be distinguished thus; in that Societies for Reformation bent their utmost Endeavours from the first to suppress publick Vice, while the Religious Societies endeavoured chiefly to promote a due Sense of Religion in their Breasts, tho' they have since been eminently instrumental in the publick Reformation. The former endeavoured to take away the Reproach of our Religion by curbing the Exorbitancies of its Professor; the latter attempted to retrieve that holy Vigour in the Practice of Religion, which becomes Christians. [10]

The societies for the Reformation of Manners tended to be led by the laity and include non-Anglicans. Yet, in reality, the differences seem slight, for, according to a contemporary source, the *Account of the Societies for Reformation of Manners in England and Ireland* (we know the fifth edition was published in 1701) such societies were also for those with a "zeal for God and religion" and who wished, in addition to "countermining the contrary attempt of all wicked men," to "recover the power as well as form of religion."

There was thus a strong holiness aspect; the *Account* states that "These persons meet often to pray, sing Psalms, and read the Holy Scriptures together, and to reprove, exhort, and edify...." [11] Often the same people were in both types of society. Some saw the Reformation of Manners also as help to return to primitive Christianity, and even Horneck agreed that the two were complimentary.

Similarities Between Anglican Societies and Pietist *Collegia*

There were many similarities between the religious societies and the Pietist *collegia*. Both were started by lay initiative, followed by clerical direction and guidance. Both types of groups sought deeper piety, stressed mutual love and support, emphasized self-examination to achieve holiness and both were loyal to the institutional church, seeking its renewal.

The *collegia*, however, certainly in the Spenerian model after 1675 as well as in many other cases, did have a greater emphasis on the study of Scripture. Furthermore, the societies did not emphasize rebirth or conversion. They assumed that to be a baptized Anglican implied conversion. The societies were also explicitly for charitable acts.

An Assessment of Societies

The Anglican societies were often small in size. They were more formal bodies than many of the cell groups encountered in other churches, with written constitutions and the like; some of them grew large and perhaps became more akin to that which today might be called a parachurch ministry than cell groups within the church.

It should be noted, however, that even where the number of members became large there was still, at times, a division into smaller groups. Contemporary accounts from the 1730's show that some societies met at 6 a.m. on Sundays for communion in one or two churches, after which they attended their own parish churches. Later that day, they would meet in small groups to pray. For many, mutual confession of sin and care for one another was at the core.

Considerable achievements can be ascribed to the societies. By 1714, around 27 percent of the Anglican churches in London had received help from them in some form. In 1707, sixty-four charity schools within ten miles of London had been established by the Society for the Promoting of Christian Knowledge (SPCK). By 1750, there were 433 societies in Wales and regions bordering England. Historians give the credit to the societies for much of the impetus for the religious awakenings that took place in England in the eighteenth century. Finally it should be noted that the societies had a profound impact on the Wesleys, as will be shown later.

As they both flourished around the same time, was there a connection between the societies and the continental Pietists? Evidence shows that there was indeed. Horneck was German and had known Labadie and Spener. Spener, in turn, knew of the English societies; his production of a Latin edition of *Pia Desideria* was partly to reach them. Francke was a member of the SPCK, which, in turn, supported the missionaries he sent out from Halle.

CHAPTER SEVEN

The Company of the Blessed Sacrament

A Roman Catholic Network of Small Groups?

All other examples in this book concern non-Roman Catholic movements in the church. Catholicism, however, has also had examples of movements of small groups. In particular, mention should be made of the *Company of the Blessed Sacrament* in France, not least because it was to have a profound influence on John Wesley in the eighteenth century.

The desire for the restoration of New Testament Christianity

In 1627, a French nobleman, Henri de Levis, Duc de Ventadour, found a deep faith in Christ and began to ponder how the Catholic élite of France might work together to promote the kingdom of God using their connections and influence. He particularly wished to see the restoration of New Testament Christianity.

The result of his thinking led to the founding in 1630 of the *Company of the Blessed Sacrament*, which became a society of laymen (later admitting women too), mainly nobles and influential people such as lawyers, with the aim, as described by a contemporary, M. Adrien Bourdoise, of reviving "the spirit of the early Christians...to profess to be like Christ by works and by holiness of life, doing all good works for the glory of God and the salvation of their neighbour." [1]

Groups began to meet on Thursdays to pray and meditate on the Scripture and other writings, particularly Kempis' *Imitation of Christ* and Lorenzo Scupoli's *Spiritual Combat*. Members fasted, visited the sick and those in prison and gave of their wealth to the poor. One of their circulars stated that the Company aimed "to do as much good as possible and to remove as much evil as possible."

Gaston de Renty

One of the first members was a nobleman and state counselor, Gaston de Renty (1611-49). He turned his castle into a hostel for scurvy sufferers, gave much to charity and preached and ministered to workmen and peasants. He wrote a pious book entitled *Twelve Rules of the Interior Life.* It is his name which is usually associated with this movement as, after the death of the founder, de Renty became the leader for some eleven years (1639-1649). He developed it into a network of some 50 groups meeting around France, with several thousand members.

These groups prayed, studied Scripture, sought to rid themselves of all that would hinder their growth into deeper holiness, seeking to obtain perfection. De Renty wrote: "We must die to the World, search out the Hindrances it brings to our Perfection."[2] To aid this sanctification process the rules of the society quite clearly state that members were to correct their brethren and point out issues in each other's lives where holiness was lacking; all should receive such admonishments willingly.

De Renty had a true love for God and was zealous that others would find God as he had done. The deep devotional life was turned outward in service; schools were founded and medical work was financed so that surgeons were able to provide free surgery for the poor.

In addition, the Company financed mission work among the North American Indians, as well as in Ireland and the Scottish isles. A contemporary letter writer judged de Renty's activities as follows: "Wherever he came he hath wonderfully advanced all Works of Piety."

Not satisfied merely in doing good they, with crusading zeal, set about exposing evil, such as reporting pimps to the police, exposing immoral priests and seeking to have people disbarred from public office if they thought them unfit. In so doing, and because of the very secretive nature of their meetings, they made many enemies, often powerful enemies who eventually brought the French Parliament around in 1660 to forbidding associations which did not hold a royal warrant. The company came within this category and dissolved itself.

De Renty influences the Puritans and Wesley

De Renty's work became influential largely due to a biography by John Baptist Saint-Jure, *The Holy Life of Monr. de Renty, a late Nobleman of France, and some time Councellor to King Lewis the 13th.* This was published in English in 1658 and impacted Puritan believers at the time, who invoked his name to justify many of their own practices.

While at Oxford, John Wesley discovered this biography and issued an abridgment in 1741, *An Extract of the Life of Monsieur de Renty,* which passed through six editions in Wesley's lifetime. It is likely that Wesley was particularly influenced in the area of the growth in holiness towards perfection, and the outworking of the devotional into social action.

A final comment

With these seventeenth century French Roman Catholic groups, we see the desire to return to the early church, the desire for personal holiness which should lead to mission and social action. While not knowing their exact position on the issue of universal priesthood, nonetheless laity were released to ministry through them. They were not seeking to be the true church within the larger church but to provide opportunities for spiritual growth and good works. They were akin to the Anglican societies.

CHAPTER EIGHT

The Moravians

Count Nicolaus Ludwig von Zinzendorf (1700-1760), an aristocrat raised in a Pietist Lutheran family and in Pietist educational institutions, allowed the settlement in 1722 of religious refugees from Moravia and Bohemia (a remnant of the *Unitas Fratrum* or *Unity of the Brethren* church) on his lands in Saxony, later to be called Herrnhut. A religious community developed in the succeeding years, with strong small group structures. In time, the Moravians became the largest Protestant missionary movement in the world to that date.

Theological Background to Small Groups

As theological background to the deployment of small groups, a few points are of relevance. Firstly, Moravianism was highly experiential, emphasizing not "rebirth" or conviction leading to repentance but rather the joy of knowing Christ, (*Glückseligkeit* in German). There was a strong emphasis on the priesthood of all believers, with people serving according to gifts. This allowed for the release of women to ministry and leadership responsibilities within their community.

The Moravians' understanding of church provided the framework for their use of small groups. The universal church consisted of true believers in all churches and denominations, the "Congregation of God in the Spirit." The local congregation was the "little flock of the wounded Lamb."

Like Spener, the Moravians stressed the organic and communal nature of the church. There were wheat and tares in the visible church whereas the invisible was the people of God in every church who could be recognized by their adherence to New Testament characteristics.

Such an understanding led Zinzendorf and the Moravians to send teams throughout Christendom to promote renewal and unity and to establish groups of like-minded people wherever they went.

These were the *Diaspora Societies* and consisted of people, remaining in their church, but meeting together in small groups for edification and renewal. If these groups were outside the Moravian community, there was also the formation of small groups within their movement for the fostering of similar objectives: these were the bands and the choirs.

These various small groups received the emphasis that they did as the Moravian view of Christianity was essentially a communal one, where unity, holiness and intimate fellowship went hand in hand. Zinzendorf once said: "I am not willing to see Christianity without community." [1] Indeed the Moravians saw that intimate community had missiological implications, that is that it would be attractive to the unbelievers and cause them to want to come to Christ:

> the blessed, fruitful, and almost irresistible "calling in" of many thousands of souls presupposes a little flock in the house which cleaves to the Saviour with body and soul, souls which are already there, united with the Saviour, so that one may point to these very people with the finger when one wants to invite others. It is an advantage, a blessing, a sound preaching of the Gospel when one can say, "Come, everything is ready. I can show you the people, who are already there; just come and see".... Thus a preaching of the Gospel must come out of this little flock: "Come, everything is ready; the time to come is here. Whoever comes now, comes at the right time." This is very simply that which is called preaching the Gospel. [2]

Three Kinds of Small Groups

Zinzendorf had grown up in a Pietist household and had been used to *collegia* meetings. While being educated at school in Halle, he started seven such groups himself among his fellow students. While studying at Wittenberg, he used his contacts to form the *Order of the Grain of Mustard Seed,* which was to seek the welfare of others and to work for the conversion of the Jews and heathen. Early in the development of his groups, therefore, it is possible to see the desire to reach out to those who did not know Christ, even to those overseas.

In the 1720's, he led a Sunday afternoon *collegium* in his home in Berthelsdorf, where the morning sermon was discussed. In 1723, together with Friedrich von Watteville, Johannes Rothe and Melchior Schaeffer he established the "Covenant of the Four Brethren" for the establishing of other groups focused on godliness and for the supporting of evangelists. When the community at Herrnhut became organized with Zinzendorf at its head, especially from 1727, it is possible to see a very defined use of cell groups.

1. Bands

The first cell groups to be organized were in July 1727, called *Banden* (bands) and later *kleine Gesellschaften* (little societies). These were originally just two or three people, later comprising between five and nine. Members were of the same sex and marital status; participation was voluntary.

People chose to associate with those whom they trusted. Initially they met weekly, but as time progressed, they tended to meet more frequently, at times even daily. Meetings were usually for one hour but could last three hours if the members so desired. Band meetings were held outdoors or in homes, but not in church buildings. Minutes were usually kept. There was considerable fluidity of membership, which was encouraged as this fostered the goal of everyone within the community being familiar with others.

Furthermore, disciplinary expulsion was employed when necessary: "I expelled Voigten from the band due to his unreliability and lack of openness" wrote Martin Dober, a band leader, in his diary of January 4, 1733. At times whole groups were disbanded if not fulfilling their function. It is possible for us to know so much of the detail of what actually took place in band meetings as minutes were kept and placed in the community's official diaries (available in German).

The bands flourished, spreading to nearby towns and even to the universities of Jena and Tübingen. By 1732, Herrnhut had five hundred residents and seventy-seven bands; in 1733 there were eighty-five bands and by 1734, one hundred.

John Wesley, on his visit in 1738, wrote in his journal that he found "about ninety bands, each of which meets twice at least, but most of them three times a week, to 'confess their faults one to another, and pray for one another, that they may be healed.'"

The Herrnhut official diary describes the inception of the bands was due to the lack of deep fellowship and lack of discussion concerning one's personal walk with God otherwise taking place. Groups were formed among those with the deepest mutual trust (hence the importance of the voluntary principle). For Zinzendorf, an honest and open speaking of one's spiritual state was necessary; these groups were to foster that need:

> Tell one another sometimes how it stands with their heart. For that is the only Way to get an upright and honest Flock, viz. to habituate them to express the true and proper Sense of their Mind; or at least, certainly not to pretend such a Thing, if it be not indeed so.[3]

Zinzendorf described the bands as those:

> who converse on the whole state of their hearts and conceal nothing from each other, but who have wholly committed themselves to each other's care in the Lord...cordiality, secrecy and daily intercourse is of great service to such individuals and ought never to be neglected.

The bands also provided the Herrnhut community with a useful and efficient way of providing pastoral care; the records show us that if someone did not attend care was taken to ascertain if all was well with them. The bands also helped ensure that practical needs were met, such as the following example from the diaries:

> In Anne Lene's band, as they were speaking of mercy, and the poor sister Christelin Paulin was present, Frau Kleinin took out a brand new frock from the cupboard and gave it to this sister in need.[4]

The bands, furthermore, played a vital role in maintaining the stability and health of the wider community. In addition to self-disclosure, the contemporary reports of band meetings show that members of the Band were free to bring their observations of one another and confront in love.

Biblical justification for bands

The Moravians had three biblical and theological justifications for bands. Firstly, the biblical pericope of Mary's visit to Elizabeth (Luke 1:39), the text used for preaching on July 2, 1727. Spangenberg (1704-1792), Zinzendorf's co-leader and eventual successor, comments that:

> Mary's visit to Elizabeth, which is remembered this day in Christendom, and the divine movement which these two sisters felt on that occasion in their, as yet hidden, children, have been brought by them [the Moravians] into gatherings of God's children, at which the Saviour is always the third man, and into the *Banden* and *Gesellschaften*... [5]

Whenever two believers were to gather, Christ would be there as the "third man," and bands were recovering the spiritual dynamic as experienced in this passage of the Bible.

Secondly, we find Zinzendorf providing biblical justification for mutual confession, from Galatians 6:1-2 and James 5:16. Zinzendorf, therefore, saw the formation of bands as a return to the New Testament practice.

Thirdly, Zinzendorf believed that Jesus often chose to work in small groups:

> But we must always remain with a small number. He called the twelve, he withdrew with his disciples, that is twelve people without sisters, and even reduced this to a group of four on Tabor and on the Mount of Olives, and finally to three when he was on the cross. [6]

Leadership of the bands

Each group had a leader and co-leader, appointed by lot, or by the groups themselves, or by Zinzendorf. Leaders were often responsible for more than one band. They met in a *Bandenkonferenz* or group leaders' meeting where they discussed problems arising in their groups. At times they would take these matters directly to Zinzendorf. Leaders also met the band members individually; such discussions remained confidential and were not to be brought to the group. Leadership could be chosen according to length of service rather than gift. The official diaries state:

The band leader does not always need to be the best in the band but only one who has been in it longer and is used to the work of the band. [7]

The role of the band leader was laid down in the diary of 1735 as watching over souls, visiting them outside band meetings, keeping confidentialities and setting an example in attendance at prayer and worship.

Initially Zinzendorf spent much of his time as "cell leader supervisor," meeting group leaders individually for supervision, asking them to account for their work. At times, a whole group might appear before him. As the number of groups increased, and as Zinzendorf's travels became more extensive, the monthly *Bandenkonferenz* or group leaders' meeting, became the main form of supervision.

Decline of the bands

The bands functioned well for around ten years before beginning to lose purpose and to decline. This was due to a number of factors; in 1737 there was a royal decree banning *Banden* (although the Herrnhuters thereafter called them *Gesellschaften*); a large number left Herrnhut for missionary work; but, most importantly, Zinzendorf himself was no longer at Herrnhut from March 1736. None proved his equal in administering a multitude of groups in a cohesive way.

2. Choirs

A second level of communal grouping within Herrnhut was the system of "Choirs," ("Chore" in German). These were larger than the bands, which became smaller divisions within the choirs. The first began among the single members in 1727, who saw the need to provide some form of communal living system, in effect fictive kinship groups.

In 1728, the Single Brethren's Choir had twenty-six members, in 1733, ninety. In 1730, the Single Sisters' choir had eighteen members, in 1734, sixty-two and in 1742, one hundred and twenty. This structure of communal living later developed among those married and among the children.

By the 1740's, there were ten choirs; the married, widowers, widows, single brothers, single sisters, older boys, older girls, little boys, little girls and infants in arms. In the Moravian communal settlement in

Bethlehem, Pennsylvania, babies, at age eighteen months, were given over to the care of the nursery, where they then lived; boys and girls entered the little boys' and girls' choirs at age four, graduating to the older boys' and girls' choirs at about twelve. Entrance to the single sisters' and brothers' choirs was around the age of nineteen. Advancement, however, was always dependent on the level of readiness or maturity of the person concerned. They were so arranged due to Zinzendorf's belief that God worked differently in different stages of one's life; he was attempting to find the structure that would allow God the optimum way of working His purposes. There was an attempt to match the instruction and Bible study passages for the choirs with their stage in life; those married were encouraged to look on Christ as the bridegroom of His bride, the Church; single brethren studied Christ in the wilderness and the itinerant ministry; boys meditated on Christ in the temple and in the carpenter's shop.

It was believed that such divisions would keep Jesus central at all times. Other matters which might rival Jesus in people's affections, such as families and relationships with the opposite sex, were thus de-emphasized. This was particularly true of the adolescent period when the Moravians realized people were at their most fertile for religious conversion. The choir ate together, worshipped together and worked together.

Choirs—the forerunner of today's affinity cells

While growing larger in size than cell groups today, these choirs were in some way the forerunner of affinity cells today (youth, women etc.).

Communal aspects of Moravian groups

There were three aspects to the bands and choirs which were absent from all other groups surveyed in this study. Firstly, they were residential and communal. This could bring great depths of fellowship, as well as inter-personal difficulties.

Secondly, there was an economic dimension, even motive, behind the groups' formation. These not only provided fictive kinship and helped develop personal spiritual life, they enabled people and the community to subsist cheaply.

Thirdly, and related particularly to the second, is the missiological dimension of the bands and choirs. The Moravians had a profound commitment to take the gospel to those who had never heard of Jesus and their whole structure facilitated this. Children could be safely left behind to be cared for in the choir, as could elder relatives; money could be provided by those remaining behind to work.

In Bethlehem, Pennsylvania, for example, in 1759, thirty-six percent of the male labor force were missionaries, supported by the remainder of the community. Weinlick has commented that the communal system at its various levels provided Moravian missionaries with a freedom of movement "second only to the celibate missionaries of Roman Catholicism." [8] Certainly the Moravians sent the biggest missionary force in the history of the Protestant church to that date, often taking small group structures with them to those newly converted, as Spangenberg recommended they do.

3. Diaspora Societies

The third type of small group advocated by the Moravians was the Diaspora Society. These societies were established as missionaries traveled through Christian lands seeking to bring together groups of believers for fellowship and unity.

Each group consisted of people from one denomination, but they were linked together in a broad ecumenical network. At such meetings, usually in homes, there was prayer, singing, reading and discussion of sermons (often Zinzendorf's), but not the Lord's supper, nor the study of Scripture so as not to encourage individualistic interpretations which might encourage separatist tendencies.

They were very similar to the Spenerian *collegia pietatis,* that is, for mutual edification rather than theological disputes. However, they were ecumenical in scope and intent. In 1745, one hundred and fifty-nine such societies had been formed in the Baltic alone, of which eighty-eight were Lutheran, thirty-eight Reformed, thirty Moravian and three others.

Specific examples in the historical records show such groups organized by Christian David and Timotheus Fiedler in the Baltic region in 1729. In 1736, in Urbs, Estonia, the local pastor, Johann Christian Quandt, held class meetings in his home; so many attended that he had to classify them according to their spiritual maturity.

In fact, revival spread around the Baltic in the 1730's, and the Moravians helped establish many cell groups. Christian David is to be found again among the Letts in 1739, establishing bands and choirs. Zinzendorf sent Friedrich Wilhelm Biefer to Basel in Switzerland in 1738. Biefer experienced a small revival with between five and six hundred Swiss being converted. These were established into thirty-two cell groups. Biefer was in fact forced to leave, whereupon he spent three months in Geneva and founded a further six cells.

In the same year, Zinzendorf himself traveled to Berlin. As clergy denied him access to the churches, he used his house for meetings; men came on Sundays and Wednesdays, women on Tuesdays and Thursdays.

Diaspora societies were also established in Frankfurt, Copenhagen, Sweden and England (the Fetter Lane Society being the most well-known example thereof). At the Synod of Zeist in 1746, it was reported that the *Unitas Fratrum* stood in connection with 540 societies, not including the 159 in the Baltic. Moravian bands and classes fostered a spiritual passion which included a commitment to missions. This, in turn, led to the formation of many other cell groups in the lands to which their missionaries went.

Influences on the Moravians' Use of Small Groups

It is quite clear that one of the main influences on the Moravian use of small groups was that of the Pietists, especially Spener. Zinzendorf grew up in a Pietist home and educational institutions, forming his own groups as a boy. Zinzendorf, moreover, was deeply impressed by the *Schlossecclesiola* (palace small group!) he experienced during a stay at the Ebersdorf palace in 1721. It was specifically this which Zinzendorf later said was the basis for his system at Hernnhut.

The Moravians themselves may have brought with them an inheritance of small groups for the early *Unitas Fratrum* employed them. In fact, in the sixteenth century, there was much correspondence between Bucer and the *Unitas Fratrum*, the latter's representatives even visiting Bucer in Strasbourg. There was much agreement on their understanding of church.

In addition, it is possible to detect specifically the influence of Jan Amos Comenius of the *Unitas Fratrum*, or at least close parallels to his beliefs. Comenius was the great leader, theologian and educationalist of the Unity of the Brethren in the seventeenth century. He stressed that the didactic process had parallels with the growth of living organisms and that appropriate content and method needed to be applied to each age and stage in a person's development. This is remarkably similar to Zinzendorf's thoughts behind the choir system. Zinzendorf's charter for the regulation of the Herrnhut community was also very close to Comenius' *Ratio Disciplinae* (1616), a copy of which Zinzendorf discovered in the library at Zittau in 1727. Also, Zinzendorf was influenced by Luther's thoughts on small groups. While in Philadelphia in 1737, Zinzendorf actually drafted a structure for the church there based on Luther's *Preface to the German Mass*.[9]

Moravian accomplishments

Over many decades of the eighteenth century, the Moravian system of small groups worked well; spiritual life was fostered, communal support was provided and many were released into the world missionary thrust, as well as local ministry and leadership. Zinzendorf succeeded in involving a whole church in foreign missions, and going far beyond others in his use of lay people as missionaries and also as preachers and church leaders. His system of bands and choirs was central to this achievement.

Other groups helped bring about aspects of ecumenical unity, hitherto unknown. Much of the above, however, was accomplished through the unusual circumstance of a residential community. The same communal dynamism proved hard to reproduce in successive generations, and, after a period of declension, communal life eventually disappeared.

CHAPTER NINE

The Methodists

John Wesley (1703-1791) was the founder of the Methodist movement which began in Great Britain in the eighteenth century. As many came to faith in Christ, Wesley and his co-leaders established a vast and interlocking network of cell groups to turn these raw converts into mature disciples and many into leaders. From the first meeting of the first group of students at the University of Oxford in 1729 until his death in 1791, Wesley tirelessly preached Christ and founded multiplying small groups. By 1791, there were 72,000 Methodists in Great Britain and 57,000 in America. By 1798, a few years after Wesley's death, there were over 100,000 members of Methodists societies in Great Britain. Around one in thirty adult men in England was a Methodist. The role of cell groups was crucial in the building of this movement of Christian disciples.

Development of Small Groups in Oxford

The 1720's found John Wesley at Oxford, first as a student and from 1725 as a teaching fellow. Wesley's main aim, however, was that he and others should attain godliness. This was succinctly expressed (1734) in a letter to his father: "My one aim in life is to secure personal holiness, for without being holy myself I cannot promote real holiness in others."

To facilitate the accomplishment of this goal, Wesley met with a small group of like-minded friends, soon known as the Holy Club: Bob Kirkham, William Morgan, John and his brother Charles. They first met in June 1729, with regular meetings from November. By March 1730, they were meeting three times weekly, reading the Latin classics; additionally, on Sunday evenings, they read theological and devotional works (such as Milton, Prior and de Renty).

In 1731, they began visiting the poor and prisoners; by August 1732, they were meeting almost daily, all together on Sundays but often at other times in smaller groups. It was in this year that a more conscious design for the multiplication of groups (at this stage still among the various colleges which formed Oxford university) fell into place, largely under the influence of John Clayton. They were "to fall upon all their friends, by which means I hope in God we shall get at least an advocate for us, if not a brother and fellow labourer, in every College in town." [1]

The focus had changed to a study of the Greek New Testament and the reading of devotional writings. At this time, the core was a group of seven but others did attend from time to time. By 1734, there were some two dozen in a number of small cells around the university; Wesley was in meetings almost every night. There was now a greater emphasis on prayer, fasting, meditation and Scripture reading. In 1735, there were about forty-five members representing some eight colleges.

John Gambold, a member of the Oxford groups stated: "But the chief business was to review what each had done that day, in pursuance of the common design, and to consult what steps were to be taken next." With the Holy Club, Wesley went further than the religious societies of the day; he was not satisfied with Bible reading and cognitive acquisition but stressed practical application, drawing up strategies of implementation and evaluation.

Development of Small Groups in Georgia

In 1735, John and Charles Wesley, with two other friends, sailed for Georgia where John wished to engage in missionary work among the Indians as well as to go on a personal spiritual quest.

Wesley's groups in Oxford had been for eager young men. In Georgia, he introduced cell group principles to a church congregation. His journal of April 1736 (Journal I:197-205) describes the situation thus:

> Not finding as yet any door open for the pursuing our main design (ministering to the Indians), we considered in what manner we might be most useful to the little flock at Savannah. And we agreed (1) to advise the more serious among them to form themselves into a sort of little society, and to meet once or

twice a week, in order to reprove, instruct, and exhort one another. (2) To select out of these a smaller number for a more intimate union with each other which might be forwarded, partly by our conversing singly with each, and partly by inviting them all together to our house; and this, accordingly, we determined to do every Sunday in the afternoon.

It is possible to see here the development to a multi-level structure of groups. His report to the Society for the Promoting of Christian Knowledge of February 1737 gives a good understanding of these groups:

some time after the Evening Service [on Sunday afternoon], as many of my parishioners as desire it meet at my house (as they do likewise on Wednesday evening) and spend about an hour in prayer, singing, reading a practical book, and mutual exhortation. A smaller number (mostly those who desire to communicate the next day) meet here on Saturday evening; and a few of these come to me on the other evenings, and pass half an hour in the same employments. [2]

In the summer of 1736, he traveled to Frederica and began cell meetings there too:

We began to execute at Frederica what we had before agreed to do at Savannah. Our design was, on Sundays in the afternoon, and every evening after public service, to spend some time with the most serious of the communicants in singing, reading and conversation. This evening we had only Mark Hird. But on Sunday, Mr. Hird and two more desired to be admitted. After a psalm and a little conversation, I read Mr. Law's Christian Perfection and concluded with another psalm. [3]

This Frederica group seems to have comprised around five or six people, mainly young women.

The Fetter Lane Society, London

Upon his return to England in 1738, Wesley was looking for suitable fellowship; this he found through his close relationship with the London Moravian leader, Peter Boehler. Together they began the Fetter Lane Society. This met weekly for prayer and confession. Within a few months, the society consisted of fifty-six men in eight bands and eight women in two bands. Monthly love feasts were held and members made financial contributions. The society met on Wednesday evenings and the bands twice weekly.

The society was, in effect, congregational in form. The members, not the leaders, decided who should be admitted or expelled, although members were placed into bands, rather than selecting them themselves. The purpose of meeting was confession of faults and mutual prayer for healing; this took place through interrogation by a leader. To aid the sanctification process, much prayer and fasting was expected.

The Fetter Lane Society had many parallels with Anglican societies, but, unlike the societies, membership was not restricted to members of the Church of England. There was no mention in the rules of the need to attend public worship; more stress was placed on continual intercession and also on the extreme importance of each member personally sharing their religious experiences. These features showed it beginning to take a different direction from the classic Anglican society.

Wesley's involvement with the Fetter Lane Society lasted only some 18 months. During that time, he had been involved in field-preaching in Bristol and elsewhere and had witnessed many of the poor turning to Christ and needing on-going instruction. He was now busy establishing groups for them. He was, moreover, increasingly unsettled about the Fetter Lane Society. His concerns particularly related to its inability to bring in the newly evangelized or affect social change, the congregational aspect of its decision-making, as well as aspects of Moravian theology.

The Foundery Society and development of Methodist small groups

Eventually he, along with twenty-five men (one third of the membership) and forty-eight women (the majority of the membership) left the society and in 1739 formed their own, calling it the Foundery Society after the building in which they met ("Foundery" being the eighteenth century spelling of "foundry"). The Fetter Lane Society in effect became the Moravian church in London.

The Foundery Society was based in Moorfields to the east side of the city of London, where Wesley would preach in the open air, giving early morning Scripture teaching before people went to work. By June

1740, there were over three hundred members in the society. He attempted to form people into bands but was dissatisfied with the small numbers participating in them.

June 1741 saw the beginning of the class meetings. In addition, Wesley introduced select societies and penitent bands, thus, in all, providing a networked system of five different group structures.

Wesley's Small Group Network

In 1748, Wesley wrote *A Plain Account of the People called Methodists* (available in *Works* VIII:248-268) which provides us with much of our understanding of his thinking behind his formation of the various groups. A number of sections will be included below as we seek to understand this phenomenon of interlocking groups.

1. Societies

The societies were all the Methodists in a given area, rather like a congregation, although non-members could attend meetings. Wesley's definition of a society, given in *A Plain Account*, was:

> a company of men having the form, and seeking the power, of godliness; united, in order to pray together to receive the word of exhortation, and to watch over one another in love, that they may help each other to work out their salvation.

The chief purpose was cognitive instruction; seats were in rows, a prepared talk was delivered; there was no response or feedback. Society meetings were arranged so as not to clash with parish church services.

It was here that Methodist theology, such as human perfectibility and the freedom of the human will were taught. Teaching was from full-time, lay preachers who were supported financially by the societies. We know that by 1744 there were 35 lay preachers. Local preachers were also used, while others served in capacities such as steward (distributing goods to the poor), or lay assistants (administration). The societies were placed into "circuits" of which there were seven in 1746 and one hundred and fourteen at the time of Wesley's death.

The largest meetings of a society tended to be on Sunday evenings. Ethical outworking of faith was stressed. The Foundery Society, for example, developed a school, gave alms to the poor, provided a dispensary for those unable to afford a doctor and published books.

In 1743, John and Charles Wesley wrote a definitive set of rules for a Methodist society which is included in this book as Appendix One (page 91).

2. Class Meetings

Class meetings became the cornerstone of Wesley's method. The term derives from the Latin *classis* meaning *division*. Wesley had grown dissatisfied with his existing system of pastoral supervision; he witnessed the regression of many who had responded to his field preaching and was at pains to provide a solution. The idea of class meetings came unexpectedly in a different context, namely that of seeking a way of covering debts incurred by the societies, as Wesley explained in *A Plain Account*:

> At length, while we were thinking of quite another thing, we struck upon a method for which we have cause to bless God ever since. I was talking with several of the Society in Bristol (February 15th, 1742) concerning the means of paying the debts there, when one stood up and said: "Let every member of the Society give a penny a week, till all are paid." Another answered: "But many of them are poor, and cannot afford to do it." "Then," said he, "put eleven of the poorest with me, and if they can give nothing, I will give for them as well as for myself; and each of you call upon eleven of your neighbours weekly; receive what they give, and make up what is wanting." It was done. In awhile some of them informed me they found such and such a one did not live as he ought. It struck me immediately, "This is the thing, the very thing we have wanted so long." I called together all the leaders of the classes (so we used to term them and their companies), and desired that each would make a particular inquiry into the behaviour of those whom he saw weekly. They did so. Many disorderly walkers were detected. Some turned from their evil ways, and some were put away from us.

Having been developed in Bristol, where the 1,100 society members were placed in classes of twelve, Wesley implemented, in April 1742, the same design in London. From this point, it was no longer possible to be a member of a society unless also a member of a class. The 426 members in London (plus 201 on trial) were divided into sixty-five classes.

By December 1743, all 2,200 members were in classes. Class meetings were formed according to geographic location; they consisted of both men and women, and people of different social backgrounds, ages and maturity in the Christian faith. Initially they met in homes, shops, attics; at a later stage, as the Methodists owned or constructed their own buildings, in small rooms on the premises. The format was usually the singing of a hymn, the leader's opening with a statement as to his spiritual condition, followed by others so doing, including testimony or admission of sin. Visitors could attend, but every other meeting was only for the members; after two visits one had either to join or cease to attend.

Wesley noted that where he merely preached, the seed fell by the wayside, but where classes were established there was lasting fruit. *A Plain Account* states:

> By the blessing of God upon their endeavors to help one another, many found the pearl of great price. Being justified by faith, they had "peace with God, through our Lord Jesus Christ." These felt a more tender affection than before, so those who were partakers of like precious faith; and hence arose such a confidence in each other, that they poured out their souls into each other's bosom.... Indeed they had a great need to do so; for the war was not over, as they had supposed; but they had still to wrestle both with flesh and blood, and with principalities and powers: so that temptations were on every side; and often temptations of such a kind, as they knew not how to speak in class; in which persons of every sort young and old, men and women, met together.

The societies became the sum total of the classes and bands; the primary point of belonging was the class. Tickets were issued; they were the entrance permits to society meetings. They were renewable quarterly; lack of attendance at class meetings excluded one from receipt of a ticket for the next quarter's meetings. Such exclusion was for the edification of those concerned that they might repent or turn again more fully to Christ. Wesley wrote in his journal of December 9, 1741 (Journal II:517):

> God humbled us in the evening by the loss of more than thirty of our little company, whom I was obliged to exclude, as no longer adorning the gospel of Christ. I believe it best to openly declare both their names and the reasons why they were excluded. We all cried unto God that this might be for their edification, and not for destruction.

Specific acts leading to exclusion from meetings included lying, smuggling, drunkenness, cursing, quarreling and wife beating. Others, of course, left of their own volition, for reasons such as their local Anglican priest's refusing them the Sacrament, their parents being against their attendance, their being mocked or losing their poor allowance.

The primary purposes of classes were discipleship and discipline, but they were also evangelistic; more professed conversion in class meetings than in the preaching services.

3. Bands

These were small groups of the same sex, same marital status and of similar age. Wesley's goal for Methodism was "to spread scriptural holiness throughout the land"; this was to entail both ethical morality and inward purity. The classes were to deal with the former; the bands the latter. Wesley's approach was largely to change the behavior first and the motives second. Although strongly encouraged, attendance at the bands was not compulsory (perhaps explaining why they did not multiply in the same way that the classes did). They were for the purposes of achieving "closer union" and for honest divulging of sins and temptations faced. Wesley explained their purposes in *A Plain Account:*

> These, therefore wanted some means of closer union; they wanted to pour out their hearts without reserve, particularly with regard to the sin which did still easily beset them and the temptations which were most apt to prevail over them. And they were the more desirous of this when they observed it was the express advice of an inspired writer: "Confess your faults one to another, and pray for one another, that ye may be healed."

The rules for the bands were definitively laid down by the Methodist Conference of 1744 (see Appendix Two, page 95). Bands were for those "who seem to have remission of sins." Each member was to speak in turn. Because they were strictly for believers, unlike class meetings, it was hoped that the bands would consist of maturer members than the classes, hence there was no leader who interrogated others but individual initiative in self-disclosure. Wesley, however, left little to chance, and in 1738 (*Works* VIII:272-3), drew up a list of questions to be used:

1. What known sins have you committed since our last meeting?

2. What temptations have you met with?

3. How were you delivered?

4. What have you thought, said, or done, of which you doubt whether it be sin or not?

5. Have you nothing you desire to keep secret?

No visitors were allowed in band meetings; indeed new members went through a rigorous screening process and trial period before others agreed to their admission.

Wesley's own assessment of bands reveals his deep commitment to them: "I have found by experience that one of these [people] has learned more from one hour's close discourse than ten years' public preaching!"[4]

The bands played a vital role in Wesleyan spirituality; however they did not become as widespread as Wesley had hoped. Of 2,200 members in the Foundery Society only 639 were in bands.

4. Select Societies

The Minutes of the Methodist Conference of 1744 state that membership of the select societies were "those who seem to walk in the light of God." They were chosen by Wesley to model holiness and to be trained in the doctrine and methods of Methodism. The select society was, furthermore, the cell group Wesley himself regularly attended for spiritual help. He explains the formation of select societies in *A Plain Account*:

I saw it might be useful to give some advices to all those who continued in the light of God's countenance, which the rest of their brethren did not want, and probably could not receive. So I desired a small number of such as appeared to be in this state, to spend an hour with me every Monday morning. My design was, not only to direct them how to press after perfection; to exercise their every grace, and improve every talent they had received; and to incite them to love one another more, and to watch more carefully over each other; but also to have a select company, to whom I might unbosom myself on all occasions, without reserve; and whom I could propose to all their brethren as a pattern of love, of holiness, and of good works.

All members of the select society were leaders of other groups, and this group was to be the model for them to imitate in their leadership of others. There were no rules, no leader, nor was there a prescribed format. Discussion could range from strategy to questioning Wesley about his activities or settling theological issues.

Confidentiality was to be maintained. Members were also to provide as much as they could towards a "common stock" (a sharing of resources). Due to the very confidential nature, there is little on record concerned the select societies. Records do show that there were 77 members of select societies in 1744. There were 25 men in the London select society alone in 1745, and also women were included.

5. Penitent Bands

Little is known about this type of small group. They first began in March 1741 for what the Methodist conference called "those who have made shipwreck of the faith." The primary goal was restitution to the mainstream of the society's life. There were hymns, prayers and instruction all suited to their circumstances, as was the timing of the meetings (Saturday evening) to keep them from the temptations of the local hostelry!

And yet while most of these who were thus intimately joined together, went on daily from faith to faith; some fell from the faith, either all at once, by falling into known, willful sin; or gradually, and almost insensibly, by giving way in what they called little things; by sins of omission, by yielding to heart-sins, or by not watching unto prayer. The exhortation and prayers used among the believers did no longer profit these. They wanted advice and instructions suited to their case; which as soon as I observed, I separated them from the rest, and desired them to meet me apart on Saturday evenings. —*A Plain Account*

Leadership Issues in the Small Groups

A vast network of class meetings necessitated a large number of leaders. Class leaders were almost entirely lay (both men and women): "But may not women, as well as men, bear a part in the honourable service? Undoubtedly, they may; nay, they ought; it is meet, right and their bounded duty. Herein there is no difference; 'there is neither male nor female in Christ Jesus.'" [5] The duties of the class leader were set down in *A Plain Account*:

It is the business of a Leader,

1) To see each person in his class, once a week at least, in order to inquire how their souls prosper; to advise, reprove, comfort, and exhort, as occasion may require; to receive what they are willing to give, toward the relief of the poor.

2) to meet the Minister and the Stewards of the society, in order to inform the Minister of any that are sick, or of any that are disorderly and will not be reproved; to pay the Stewards what they have received of their several classes in the week preceding.

The leader was to set the example by being the first to state the condition of his or her spiritual life. Class leaders were appointed by the society's leaders and supervised by them; they were trained and accountable. Character was the key qualification, particularly faithfulness.

Influences on Wesley's Formation of Cell Groups

A considerable number of influences are discernible on Wesley's understanding of cell groups. These include Puritanism, Pietism, the Anglican societies (particularly the example established by his father), de Renty, the Moravians and the anonymously written book of 1680, *A*

Country Parson's Advice to His Parishioners.

Wesley's mother was greatly influenced by the **Puritan** writers. She taught her children in the Puritan tradition, namely emphasizing submission of their will to God's, instilling disciplined methods, and spending one hour weekly with each child individually, inquiring into his or her spiritual life.

Wesley visited **Pietist** centers on the Continent; he also read many Pietist works such as Francke's *Pietas Hallensis* and Arndt's *True Christianity*. It is possible that Wesley saw a program of implementation in *True Christianity*; certainly Arndt's view of the differing stages of spiritual development moving towards perfection has parallels in Wesley's purposes for the formation of different groups.

Wesley was familiar with the **Societies**. In 1700, his father, Samuel Wesley, had established a small religious society in his parish of Epworth:

> First to pray to God; secondly, to read the Holy Scriptures and discourse upon religious matters for their mutual edification; and thirdly, to deliberate about the edification of our neighbour and the promoting of it. [6]

Samuel designed a mechanism for growth, and multiplication, but with strong central leadership: if more than 12 wished to join, two should begin a new group, but the rector would maintain primacy over issues of import and change. The Holy Club at Oxford was formed largely on the Society model; many of its participants attended meetings of other societies as well.

Wesley had read the biography of **de Renty**. As was shown in Chapter Seven, he was concerned with holiness of life and ministration to the poor. He advocated daily spiritual self-examination, weekly cell groups for prayer, devotions and for distribution of food to the poor, and social works, such as the provision of cheap medicines for those who could not afford doctors.

Wesley took to imitating a number of de Renty's practices, such as carrying a cloth with him so as to expunge graffiti, and used de Renty's groups as a model. Whereas Anglican societies were for personal growth with the hope that service would be the outcome, de Renty stressed that it is service which is the context in which growth occurs. This aspect was particularly appealing to Wesley.

Wesley's encounter with the **Moravians** while sailing in bad weather to Georgia is widely known. He was deeply impressed with their piety and quiet assurance in God. When in London, subsequent to his stay in the colonies, it was the Moravian leader, Peter Boehler, who was very influential in helping Wesley come to a new understanding of conversion and assurance of salvation.

Wesley was impressed by the Moravian cell groups he encountered in Georgia and London. Together, Wesley and Boehler established the Fetter Lane Society in May 1738, with Wesley, the following month visiting Herrnhut. In a letter to Herrnhut (*Journal* II:496) he wrote, "I greatly approve of your conferences and bands; of your method of instructing children; and, in general, of your great care of the souls committed to your charge."

Upon his return to England, Wesley established bands and wrote: "we are endeavouring here also, by the grace which is given us to be follower of you, as ye are of Christ." [7] The division of bands according to gender and marital status, for example, was a direct borrowing from them, as was the size of the bands, usually five to ten. Perhaps most importantly, Wesley learned from the Moravians the crucial separation between the functions of instruction and edification.

In the *London Magazine* (December 1760) Wesley wrote that the advice in the anonymous book *A Country Parson's Advice to His Parishioners* to form societies in order to restore Christianity (see Chapter Six) had been an impetus for starting the Oxford Methodist Society and others subsequently.

Primitivism lay behind much of Wesley's thinking, particularly with regard to his ecclesiology and formation of groups. He was influenced by the prevailing primitivism within Anglicanism, particularly within the societies (as shown previously). He may have also been strengthened in his looking to the early church as the role model by his encounter with the Moravians and the likes of John Clayton, who had been one of the early members of the Holy Club. The latter introduced him to the *Apostolic Constitutions* which gave primitive authority to devotions and fasts.

In Georgia, he read Beveridge's *Synodikon* which showed that even some of the early church councils went beyond Scripture and that Scripture was the more important. This led Wesley to change the basis for his ecclesiology to provide a more scriptural foundation. At this point, he moved away from the Patristic primitivism common in the religious societies to a New Testament primitivism. It was precisely the formation of cell groups which Wesley saw as part of a restoration of New Testament Christianity. In *A Plain Account* he wrote:

> But as soon as any of these [in the early church] was so convinced of the truth, as to forsake sin and seek the gospel salvation, they immediately joined them together, and met these *katacoumenoi,* "catechumens" (as there were then called), apart from the great congregation that they might instruct, rebuke, exhort, and pray with them, and for them, according to their inward necessities.

Wesley's View—
The True Church is a Community of the Converted

Clearly Wesley's implementation and use of small groups flows from his understanding of the believer and of the church. Although seeking to hold on to a more traditional Anglican, sacramental view of the church, there was much in Wesley that favored the concept of the church being only the true believers and that two or three gathering was also church. He held that the church had fallen, particularly after Constantine's baptism, and that true spirit of the church thereafter was to be found in small groups of faithful believers. Clearly he believed in lay ministry, not just for a few.

A further significant aspect to Wesley's theology is the need for conversion to Christ and assurance of salvation; conversion was the aim of preaching and the criteria of admission to the bands. The chief goal of all methodology was holiness, or Christian perfection.

This strong belief in God's grace to make this possible is a chief characteristic of Methodism: "This doctrine [of holiness] is the grand depositum which God has lodged with the people called Methodists; and for the sake of propagating this chiefly he appears to have raised us up," wrote Wesley (*Works* XIII:9); it was the prime motive behind much group dynamic. The classes were to aid holiness of behavior, the bands the inner attitudes. This perfection was, however, to be worked out in groups, not in an isolated, individual way.

This leads to a third characteristic of Wesleyan theology, the importance of the corporate, trenchantly argued for in his Preface to the 1739 Hymnbook:

Solitary religion is not to be found there [the Gospel]. "Holy solitaries" is a phrase no more consistent with the Gospel than holy adulterers. The Gospel of Christ knows of no religion, but social; no holiness, but social holiness. [8]

Wesley was, however, still aware of the power of sin, even in the believer, and therefore, made provision for confession, accountability and repentance within his system.

An Assessment of Wesley's Methodology of Small Groups

Wesley's methodology was undoubtedly effective, with 101,712 members in the societies in 1798, around one in thirty adult men in England a Methodist, many testifying to changed lives and holding responsibilities. A belief in the perfectibility of human nature, particularly worked out in intimate group fellowship and accountability were key factors in this, as well as commitment to evangelize and find appropriate vessels to contain the harvest.

Henderson [1997] posits ten methodological components to the group system which were behind its success: a hierarchy of interlocking groups; the point of entry into the system is behavioral change, followed by affective, aspirational and rehabilitative functions; constitutional authority (that is authority in the rules, not in Wesley); groups were graded by readiness; total participation and mobilization; instrumental group activities (that is, prepared questions); exclusion for non-compliance; individual care; multiple accountability; separation of cognitive, affective and behavioral functions.

The above relate to the factors within the Methodist movement (endogenous factors). There were also exogenous factors behind the success, that is, issues in the society at large. Firstly, large scale social and demographic change was taking place in the eighteenth century, with increasing industrialization and urbanization. This produced isolation and alienation among the working classes. Wesleyans were able to offer appropriate structures, values and methodologies, providing fictive kinship groups when other networks of relationships had broken down.

Secondly, there was also an increasing sense of the private self being the repository of spiritual experience, due to these sociological changes; Wesley's Arminianism suited this well as Arminianism rejected the elitists' tendencies of Calvinism and brought a more democratic, even demotic sense of salvation.

Thirdly, Methodism grew among the skilled and hard-working poor who were upwardly mobile in economic terms and thus able to contribute financially. (This is contrary to the view posited by one famous historian, E.P. Thompson, who analyzed Methodism as a "chiliasm of the defeated and the hopeless."[9]) It is clear from membership records that Methodism flourished among the skilled artisans.[10]

Fourthly, it seems that 1730-50 was a stable time in British history, certainly in economic terms, and thus an ideal time to launch a new movement. Furthermore, the wider Church of England was unable to adapt to the vast changes taking place. During the middle of the eighteenth century, Puritanism was on the decline, the High church party was damaged over political issues and the religious societies were in decline. There was, therefore, to some degree, a vacuum in British church life towards the filling of which the Methodist movement contributed vastly.

CHAPTER TEN

Observations From History

Having given an overview of those occasions within the history of the church where cell groups in their various forms were established, it seems appropriate to reflect on what this study has shown. A number of observations will, therefore, be made.

The Universality of Small Groups

Cell groups have appeared in a number of different historical, cultural, ecclesiastical and social settings.

Historical: It has been shown that small groups extend from the middle of the sixteenth century (Bucer), through the seventeenth century (Puritan and Pietist groups, the religious societies) through to the end of the eighteenth century (Wesleyan).

Cultural: Reference has been made to their occurrence in a number of cultures, namely Scandinavia, Holland, Switzerland, the Baltic states, England, Germany and France.

Denominational: Small groups were active in many different ecclesiastical traditions: Anglican, Lutheran, Reformed, independent, Moravian and Roman Catholic.

Social: It is also possible to observe that small groups existed within very differing social classes. The Anglican societies drew their strength largely from the more educated classes, while de Renty's were drawn from the élite. Pietist *collegia* varied considerably; they often flourished in prosperous trading towns, and yet many were among peasants. The Moravians were refugees, largely self-educated peasants and craftsmen. The constituency of Methodism was among the growing working classes, as Wesley remarked: "The uneducated are always a majority with us. Everywhere we find the labouring part of mankind the readiest to receive the Gospel." [1]

It seems, therefore, that God is able to bring together like-minded believers to restore some element of family unit within the church within all sectors of society. They are established among people of all social backgrounds because there a basic human need to meet in small family-like cells; that is indeed the way humans are made. Modern social scientific research makes this point, namely that small groups, referred to as "primary" groups, appear in all cultures. [2] In restoring cell groups to the church, we can be meeting one of mankind's basic needs for intimate fellowship and belonging.

Common Theological Characteristics

Despite the above diversity of location, ecclesiastical tradition and social constituency, it is possible to discern a number of common theological characteristics, perhaps not present in all those investigated, but nonetheless common to most. Certain theologies and beliefs tend to lead to the establishment and on-going support of small groups. These provide the value system in which small groups will flourish, for cell groups are not a structural exercise but the outworking in life of a deep value system. Among such theological characteristics, the following may be found.

1. A strong belief in the **corporate nature** of Christianity rather than the individual. The proponents of the religious societies saw the "benefit of their conferences one with another" in dealing with sin; [3] Zinzendorf was "not willing to see Christianity without community;" [4] Wesley knew of neither solitary religion nor solitary holiness—both were social. Bucer stressed the passages of Scripture which taught on communal life, such as Acts, chapters 2 and 4.

2. An **organic concept of church,** rather than organizational or structural. Church is seen in essence not as an organization, nor some-

thing to which all belong, nor as the building but as something living, perhaps invisible. It is body or family rather than organization. It is the coming together of believers in itself which is church, as Spener wrote: "One understands by the word "church," however, the gatherings of Christians, in general as well as in certain special groups. The former is the universal; the latter are the singular churches." Not everyone in this study would have stated it this way, but, in essence, for many there was such an organic, family understanding of church. Zinzendorf used familial vocabulary (fellow believers were "God's children") or terms of endearment (gatherings of Christians were the "little flock").

3. The **experiential nature** of the Christian faith. The religious societies wished to recover "the power as well as the form of religion."[5] Zinzendorf stressed *Glückseligkeit*, the joy of knowing Christ. Wesley described his conversion as his "heart strangely warmed."[6] God was to be experienced and lives changed; faith was not simply a matter of correct belief.

4. The **universal priesthood**. All Christians were to minister. This was stressed less in the societies, where there was greater ordained involvement. In other movements, however, this was vital to the health and life of the group. Spener, in *The Spiritual Priesthood*, wrote that all believers were to edify one another, teach and admonish. Within Herrnhut virtually all the leadership was lay, as was the majority of missionaries sent to other lands. Wesley, while still holding to the importance of ordination for some, built his movement on lay leaders and lay preachers. Methodist group multiplication would not have been achievable without lay ministry and lay leadership.

5. **Voluntarism,** that is **personal decision** to join the group, unlike membership of the territorial churches. There is, therefore, an aspect of the believers' church ecclesiology evident to some extent in all the movements in question. This is controversial, as some (Luther and Bucer, for example) would have strenuously denied their adherence to such a position; nonetheless, it is valid. In the *Preface to the German Mass,* Luther called for the gathering of those "who are desirous of being Christians in earnest, and are ready to profess the Gospel with hand and mouth."

Bucer called for the formation of "true" Christian communities who were serious in their walk with God. Furthermore, in Pietism, Moravianism and Methodism there was a clear distinction between the true believer and the non-believer. Pietism stressed either the process (*Busskampf*—the struggle resulting from conviction) or the standing (*Wiedergeburt*—rebirth) which separated the two; Moravianism stressed the resultant state after *Wiedergeburt*, namely *Glückseligkeit*, joyous blessedness; Methodism spoke of "awakened persons" or those "who seem to have remission of sins."

The believer could demonstrate his theological and juridical position by choosing to join a *collegia*, band or small group of some name. The commitment level was high, particularly in Moravianism and Methodism, with strict group boundary maintenance and expulsion for lack of participation or attendance. Whether seeking to express oneself as the true, invisible church within the visible (*ecclesiola in ecclesia*) or as some kind of sectarian movement (Methodism), some expression of the believers' church theology is evident.

6. **A developmental understanding of life, growth and sanctification** seems to underpin many of these movements and how they were structured. This was true of Bucer and of many of the Pietists. Arndt, one of the most influential of the Pietists wrote in *True Christianity*:

> As there are different stages and degrees of age an maturity in the natural life; so there are also in the spiritual. It has its first foundation in sincere repentance, by which a man sets himself heartily to amend his life. This is succeeded by a greater illumination, which is a kind of middle stage. Here, by contemplation, prayer, and bearing the cross, a man is daily improving in grace, and growing up to perfection. The last and most perfect state is that which consists in a most firm union, which is founded an cemented by, pure love. This is that state which St. Paul calls "the perfect man" and "the measure of the stature of the fullness of Christ" (Ephesians 13).

This work was to influence Wesley who discovered the text in 1736 and published extracts from it. From this understanding of human development, Wesley divided people accordingly so they could be taught and helped in line with the needs appropriate to their stage in the Christian life.

Other Pietists held similar views. The Dutchman Coornhert (1522-1590), in his *Hertspegel godlijker Schrifturen vertoonende een klare, korte ende sechere wegh,* stressed that Christians could be divided into three groups, based on 1 John 2, namely children, full-grown men who possess strength to do God's will and parents whose knowledge of Christ is such that they bring forth children.

Comenius believed in different kinds of education according to the stages in which people found themselves (*Ratio Disciplinae*). When Zinzendorf wrote in 1727 *Manorial Injunctions and Prohibitions,* he was surprised and pleased to find that his ideas resembled those of Comenius' *Ratio Disciplinae.* As Zinzendorf was to say: "God is adapting Himself to the varied ways of each man, woman and child, going his specific ways with them in each place...."

7. **Mutual lay confession,** rather than confession solely between the believer and God. While not wishing to replace an intermediary between the individual and God and holding to the Reformation doctrines, time and again we see the belief that confession to one another was important for overcoming sin and growth in holiness. In Chapter One, several examples were given of Luther's writings encouraging the mutual confession of sin. For many of the Pietist groups this was not such a feature, yet everyone was to have a spiritual father if not a group to whom they confessed. The religious societies had the aim to "better discover their own corruptions, the devil's temptations, and how to countermine his subtle devices." Furthermore, we have seen that the Moravian and Wesleyan bands most definitely engaged in mutual confession of sin and temptation.

8. The belief in **church discipline,** and that small groups were to be the place to restore an effective biblical discipline. In the *Preface to the German Mass* Luther wrote that "those whose conduct was not such as befits Christians could be recognized, reproved, reformed, rejected, or excommunicated, according to the rule of Christ in Matthew xviii."

Bucer had written in *Enarrationes in sacra quattuor evangelia* that the text of Matthew 18:15-20 implied that small communities should be created on the basis of discipline. The religious societies had strict disciplinary rules; we have seen that people could be expelled from both the Moravian bands and Wesleyan groups for such things as non-attendance, stealing, wife-beating and the like. Ethical standards were to be maintained through discipline.

Motivations for Establishing Small Groups

A number of motivations for the establishment of small groups are discernible in history.

Primitivism

This was one of the chief motivations throughout the centuries for the establishment of small groups. It was believed that the church should be restored to and modeled upon the New Testament church and that this church met in homes, having small communities and family units within it (termed *fictive kinship groups* by sociologists). Bucer was adamant that the church needed to be faithful to the apostolic times and that true communities were to restore that faithfulness. Spener wished "to reintroduce the ancient and apostolic kind of church meetings." We have seen Horneck's desire to return to the primitive church. The Moravians viewed their bands as a restoration of early church fellowship, as did Wesley, who believed the early church gathered new converts together for instruction and exhortation. The Company of the Blessed Sacrament was to revive "the spirit of the early Christians."

A further way of viewing such primitivism within the movements studied is as a profound anti-ritualism. There was a desire to cut through traditions, formulae and all intervening ritual forms which hindered the believer from experiencing God for himself. A return to the New Testament church, where it was believed there were no such rituals, was an attempt to remove all such obstructions to God and thus open the way for personal and experiential relationship with God.

Were these reformers correct in establishing small groups to return to the New Testament church? This is, of course, a vital question for us today and one to which a detailed answer is beyond the scope of this book. However, a few comments may briefly be made.

From a study of the Bible, it is possible to see that the early believers, in addition to meeting in the Temple and synagogues, also met in various homes; for example, salutations are addressed to churches meeting in homes. Furthermore, modern extra-biblical research shows that cell groups were structures within both first century society and church. The first century Graeco-Roman world had many voluntary organizations, *collegia,* often for fellowship, functioning as fictive kinship groups; society at large was based on the household (oikos). The early church was patterned after such structures. To a large measure, therefore, the movements in the centuries after the Reformation who sought the primitivistic ideal in small groups were justified in so doing. [7]

The pursuit of personal and ethical holiness

Spener encouraged *collegia* in order "to put into practice what they read [the Scriptures]." [8] Horneck's rules for societies made the resolution upon a holy life the key membership criterion. The Moravian and Wesleyan bands were for confession of sin and overcoming temptation in order live a perfect life. Throughout the different movements, there was a strong motivation to form groups to aid in the living of a holy life. Indeed perfection was the aim. Wesley wrote, "My design was, not only to direct them how to press after perfection..." De Renty wrote: "We must die to the World, search out the Hindrances it brings to our Perfection."

Ministry to those outside the group in spiritual and material need

Most groups existed either to engage in social action, societal reformation or evangelizing the lost. The societies collected money each meeting to give to the poor; they began a number of hospitals, schools and the like. De Renty's groups gave much for societal reformation and social action, as did the Methodists. The latter were also particularly evangelistic in their goals as well, whereas for the Moravians their groups became the bedrock from which to launch a missionary movement unparalleled at that time.

Church reform

Lastly, for many there was the motivation to reform the church. Bucer clearly wanted his communities to affect the whole church. The Pietist *ecclesiolae in ecclesia* principle was that the *collegia* would act as leaven to affect and purify the whole church. A similar motivation can be found among the Moravians, particularly with the Diapsora societies.

Justification for Small Groups

The chief justification for small groups was that of returning to the early church. Various passages of Scripture were employed to gain legitimization for the various attempts at small groups, but the most frequently used was the text of Matthew 18, of which verses 15-20 read:

> If your brother sins against you, go and show him his fault, just between the two of you. If he listens to you, you have won your brother over. But if he will not listen, take one or two others along, so that "every matter may be established by the testimony of two or three witnesses." If he refuses to listen to them, tell it to the church; and if he refuses to listen even to the church, treat him as you would a pagan or tax collector. I tell you the truth, whatever you bind on earth will be bound in heaven, and whatever you loose on earth will be loosed in heaven. Again, I tell you that if two of you on earth agree about anything you ask for, it will be done for you by my Father in heaven. For where two or three come together in my name, there am I with them.

This passage was employed by Luther, Bucer, and Spener and others to justify small groups and their disciplinary nature. A second widely employed text is that of James 5:16 for the mutual confession of sin and sharing of life's struggles.

CHAPTER ELEVEN

Lessons From History

Having made a number of observations from history, what lessons might we draw for today, particular for those who are seeking to employ some type of cell group ministry or participate in house churches? All the lessons have application equally to cell groups or house church; for brevity, therefore, in general only one term will be employed but the other should be understood, although specific distinctions will at times be made where necessary. A number of lessons are suggested below.

Foundational Values and Commitments for Cell Ministry

Cell groups are primarily an issue of heart values, not structure

The successful examples that have been examined flourished due to the value system and theology which lay behind them. Merely to organize one's church into cell groups for organizational or other purposes misses the point. They flourish when a correct value system is in place. (See the following point.)

Core values which allow for cell groups

These include: the priesthood of all believers (allowing for everyone to be released to minister); the desire to pursue God's holiness; an acknowledgment that the individual believer cannot walk in holiness on his or her own; accountability and openness; the church is body and family; a desire to reach the lost. Without such underlying values cell groups become another organizational or management tool, not the vessel to contain the work of God's Spirit.

In matters of personal holiness, there is power in the corporate not available to the individual

Cell groups provide a place for teaching, for questions to be asked and issues to be discussed without the fear of judgment or rejection. Cells provide encouragement and sanctions if necessary. Self disclosure brings an increase in self-awareness and social awareness. This is supported by modern psychological and sociological research, where findings point to "enhanced drive" (that is better performance) through "mere presence" or "evaluation apprehension" coming from within the group.[1] The presence of others acts as a "social facilitator." Modern research tells us that such groups are particularly effective when they concentrate on "here and now behavior."[2]

Cells are a valid and vital part of church life

Cells are not merely a temporary expediency. Some in history saw their groups as an interim measure, or "second best" until the church was restored. Others believed them legitimate in their own right. It was the latter who produced the more robust groups. Cells help meet basic human needs and were part of the early church.

Cells come from a desire to emulate the early church

Wanting to emulate the early church is a powerful and proper motivation, legitimization and justification for cell groups today.

Cells groups are trans-cultural

They can flourish in many different cultures and environments. They provide for a basic human need of belonging to a family group. This might be particularly pertinent in modern Western society where so many people are no longer in healthy family groups of any kind. The trans-cultural nature of cells also means that they are important for cross-cultural missionary work.

Cells as Part of a Wider Movement
Cells tend to be established whenever God is renewing His church.

They tend to be present in renewal movements of all kinds whether it be to establish a true believers' church, to renew an existing denomination or to create new church (the latter in effect being the outcome, whether intentional or not, of both Zinzendorf's and Wesley's reforms).[3]

Cells should be part of a network of groups

Cells should be part of a larger movement. In both Moravianism and Methodism, the cells worked well, because there was a clear relationship with sub-groups such as bands, and with the wider body, the Herrnhut community or the Wesleyan society. An isolated cell on its own tends not to flourish. A cell meeting cannot provide all that the members need. This point does apply to house churches too. Although each house church is an autonomous church, there is still huge benefit in the areas of vision, accountability and teaching if the church is part of a broader network or movement, as indeed many modern house churches are.

Cell groups flourish when their mission and identity are clear

There needs to be clear understanding and stated reasons for their existence as well as clear group boundaries. Many of the societies had rules which clearly focused participants toward goals. Within Moravianism and Methodism, each kind of group had its clearly defined function.

Sociologists take this concept further by describing a group as having "high grid" when it fits well into the wider society and "low grid" where there is difference between the group and the wider norms. Many of the movements studied demonstrated "low grid" when taken within the context of the surrounding society and/or church. This was their impetus for reform.

As a secondary perspective needs to be added, however, concerning the group or movement itself. A movement is said to experience "strong group" when there is:

high pressure to conform along with strong corporate identity, clear distinction between ingroup and outgroup, clear sets of boundaries separating the two, and a clear set of normative symbols defining, expressing, and replicating group identity.

or "weak group" when there is:

low pressure to conform along with rather nebulous group identity (individualism), fuzzy distinctions between ingroup and outgroup, highly porous sets of boundaries between interfacing groups, and few or too many non-normative symbols defining, expressing, and replicating group identity. [4]

Radical groups in the history of the church, as well as in society, tend to fit into the strong group/low grid quadrant. They experience a profound dissatisfaction with the surrounding society and church; they, therefore, wish to implement change and do so through "strong group" formation.

Bucer, the Pietist, the Anglican societies, the Moravians and the Methodists all displayed "low grid" in their perception of the church around them and all, to differing degrees, displayed characteristics of "strong group" as the vehicle for reform. The ones which were more successful, however, seem to have demonstrated a higher degree of "group strength" than others. The Methodists, for example, had clear organization, structure and leadership, clear articulation of goals and a high commitment to the groups, requiring loyalty to the society and class before other societies.

Cell group movements today would do well to build "group strength" by clearly articulating both the dissonance with surrounding environment and the aspiration of change, as well as the means to achieve that change. Rigorous group boundary maintenance is also a factor.

Cells flourished when there was a key leader who could communicate vision and articulate the purposes of the movement

Although spontaneous, the Pietist *collegia* found their aspirations articulated by Spener. The Moravians, in Zinzendorf, found a gifted leader who could point the way ahead and hold them together. Without his close oversight the bands floundered. Wesley was a master at leading a growing movement. He could articulate the aspirations of and be a trenchant apologist for eighteenth century Methodism.

The importance of writing down and publishing the cell vision

Linked with the previous point is the importance of publishing. All the movements benefited when their ideals and methods could be written and disseminated through publication.

Those who eventually began new churches seem to have greater success than those who sought to reform the old

Although none of the movements studied began wishing to establish a new church or denomination, including both Wesley and Zinzendorf, the latter two, in effect, did so. Zinzendorf could, of course, appeal that he was merely reviving the ancient *Unitas Fratrum*, and

Wesley that he was renewing the Church of England. Both, however, led a new church movement of which they were the primary leader.

Sociologists of religion speak of church and sect, taken from Troeltsch.[5] He sees the church as a more traditionalist institution; it is world-accepting; it has special officers committed to the institution; members are usually born into it; it appeals to all sectors of society, but often the higher classes. This is in contradistinction to the sect, which is voluntary, conversionist, emphasizes loving fellowship and commitment to the group, usually finding the lower classes as its constituency. Both Moravianism under Zinzendorf and Methodism were essentially sectarian in nature, whatever their leaders claimed.

In history, cell groups have multiplied and flourished under the sectarian model. The sociologist of religion, Hamilton, shows us that if the "relatively powerful" in a movement prevail, that is the educated or clergy, the movement will tend to stay within the church. However, if the "relatively dissatisfied majority" prevails, then the group tends to move sectwards.

The need for multiplication

Some of the more successful networks of cell groups had the clear goal of multiplication. The Moravians aimed to set up Diaspora societies in the nations of Europe and also among the converted on the mission field. Wesley was seeking to establish an increasing number of societies and classes to both win the lost and contain the fruit of his evangelism.

Cells and Leadership
Leaders must be developed

For cells to function, certainly if they are to multiply, there must be an adequate number of competent leaders. This is best demonstrated by the Wesleyans, who were able to see hundreds of lay men and women developed into leaders. Wesley, through his sermons and writing but perhaps particularly through the select societies was able to impart his values to others who could then, in turn, impart them to others. The training of large numbers of leaders was key for the success of Methodism.

Leaders should meet together for mutual support and learning

The preceding point also demonstrates the benefit of cell leaders gathering as leaders for mutual sharing or experiences and learning. Both the Wesleyans and Moravians saw the importance of the group leaders meeting as part of their on-going leadership development.

Leadership must be modeled

In the Wesleyan classes the leader would share his own experiences and struggles first; this would then encourage others to be open as well. Modern research validates this approach: "A person being interviewed by a high status person who serves as a model will increase the amount of self-disclosure if the model either speaks first or reinforces the person of the desired behavior." [6]

Controlling leadership stifles groups

In Pietism where there was often a fear of offending the civil authorities or of separatistic tendencies there was strict ministerial or even magisterial control. This tended to lead to a lack of effective lay participation and certainly was a constraint to multiplication. Many became frustrated and did, in fact, separate from the church.

The importance of character in the selection of leaders

This was the key criterion for Wesley and will be so if the group's purpose is growth in sanctification.

The Cell Meeting

Cell groups can and should be multi-functional

We have seen the various groups provide pastoral care, practical assistance when members are in need, discipleship, teaching, prayer, evangelism, mission and social action. Many, or indeed all, of the functions of church can be carried out at the cell level. (As mentioned earlier, there is a different understanding between modern cell churches and house churches on this point. Most cell churches still advocate congregational meetings as well as groups; house churches would not necessarily do so.)

Cells should be outwardly focused

Cells should be outwardly focused, aiming to meet the needs of those around them and further afield. The societies and de Renty's groups sought to do good works and relieve suffering, as did the Pietists and Wesleyans. The latter had the clear goal of evangelizing the lost, perhaps a chief reason why they multiplied to the extent that they did. Cells must be evangelizing and concerned for social action.

Cell groups should be open to non-believers
It was Zinzendorf's aim that the small groups would welcome unbelievers and that the very existence of such loving families would be attractive to those outside. Wesley's classes could also function similarly. Non-members were allowed to attend, at least for a while.

Cell groups should exercise discipline
A motivation for many of the groups we have studied was the provision of discipline, which the larger church body seemed unable or unwilling to provide. For the cells to work certain behavior was not permissible. Successful cells and on-going discipleship require the maintenance of standards.

Group size must be limited
The group size must be limited for intimate fellowship and sharing to occur. With a group of 50, Spener had to relinquish his goal of providing intimate fellowship. Wesley, in keeping classes and bands small, saw considerable success.

Confession and accountability work better in some kind of sub-group
Confession and accountability work better in some kind of subgroup rather than the whole cell; this sub-group should be people of the same gender. This is clearly demonstrated by the vitality and fruit of the both the Moravian and Wesleyan bands.

Cells function better in the home or informal surroundings
Bucer wished his communities to meet in the pastor's home. Spener noticed that a move from homes to a church building had a detrimental effect on his *collegium*. The Moravians insisted that the bands did not meet in a church building. The building in which the group meets can affect, either positively or negatively, the outcome of the group. This is supported by modern research, where for example, unhelpful environment has been proven to increase "cognitive fatigue" in group members. [7]

Cells should be contextualized

Contextualization is the adapting of core values and principles to fit in with the surrounding culture and society. Wesley was so successful at contextualization in his groups for eighteenth century Britain. They provided fictive kinship groups for many experiencing profound dislocation due to the vast social changes taking place, and established practices and appropriate methodologies suitable for the times, such as the issuing of tickets to attend and the like. Some of the practices would be strange in the twenty-first century. It is our task to adopt the values of cell but in culturally relevant forms.

Earlier reference was made to the anti-ritualistic nature of primitivistic groups. It may be that, as part of the contextualization process, the cell group will have to establish its own rituals to help maintain group identity, but rituals appropriate for the culture and times.

Currie [1977] asserts that churches may have little control over external factors and constituencies but that success at drawing people into the internal constituency depends on proximity, congruity and utility. Cell groups help a church or movement maintain proximity to people in that they are in neighborhoods where people live. The Methodists were particularly good at this by having circuits, itinerant preachers and the like.

Congruity is when people feel that they can join the group and yet not withdraw from the routines of their daily life. Again, this is all part of the contextualization process. Cells can do well when they fit around peoples' daily and weekly routines.

Further Lessons From History

Some specialist ministries may be required in addition to the cell

Wesley found that some people had such intractable problems and life-controlling issues that the normal society or class could not adequately deal with them; he, therefore, established specialized rehabilitative groups. Today these might be akin to the establishing of "12 step" recovery groups.

The importance of reading history and biography

Time and again it has been shown how various people in history read and learned from others, particularly those who preceded them in their quest to follow God and build His church. Many had read Luther and were able to use his writings as an apologetic; Spener gained comfort and legitimization from Bucer; Wesley read de Renty and Arndt. The Scriptures say: "Stand at the crossroads and look; ask for the ancient paths, ask where the good way is, and walk in it, and you will find rest for your souls" (Jeremiah 6:10). In many cases, leaders were influenced and encouraged by those who had gone before them as they read of how God had already led others.

Afterword

It has been the aim of this book to examine the various attempts at small groups and cell groups that were made in the history of the church in the centuries subsequent to the Reformation so that we might learn from the experience of those who have preceded us. It is hoped that this study has been both revealing and encouraging to many in the church today who are seeking to establish family units—cell groups—in their churches or indeed to establish small house churches and that from the reading of this book lessons can be learned and mistakes avoided. When God moves, small groups are established to contain His work; this is the lesson of history. May God build His church in our day as He has sought to do throughout the centuries. Amen!

Peter Bunton
Luton, England
Email: peterbunton@compuserve.com

Cell Groups and House Churches: What History Teaches Us

APPENDIX ONE

The Full Text of the Rules
of the Society of the People called Methodists

John and Charles Wesley
1st May 1743

1. In the latter end of the year 1739, eight or ten persons came to me in London, who appeared to be deeply convinced of sin, and earnestly groaning for redemption. They desired (as did two or three more the next day) that I would spend some time with them in prayer, and advise them how to flee from the wrath to come, which they saw continually hanging over their heads. That we might have more time for this great work, I appointed a day when they might all come together; which, from thenceforward, they did every week; viz. on Thursday, in the evening. To these, and as many more as desired to join with them (for their number increased daily), I gave those advices from time to time which I judged most needful for them; and we always concluded our meeting with prayer suited to their several necessities.

2. This was the rise of the United Society, first in London, and then in other places. Such a Society is no other than "a company of men having the form, and seeking the power, of godliness; united, in order to pray together, to receive the word of exhortation, and to watch over one another in love, that they may help each other to work out their salvation."

3. That it may the more easily be discerned whether they are indeed working out their own salvation, each Society is divided into smaller companies, called Classes, according to their respective places of abode. There are about twelve persons in every Class; one of whom is styled the Leader. It is his business:

(i) To see each person in his Class once a week at least, in order

To inquire how their souls prosper;

To advise, reprove, comfort, or exhort as occasion may require;

To receive what they are willing to give towards the support of the gospel:

(ii) To meet the Ministers and the Stewards of the Society once a week in order

To inform the Minister of any that are sick, or of any that walk disorderly, and will not be reproved;

To pay to the Stewards what they have received of their several Classes in the week preceding; and

To show their account of what each person has contributed.

4. There is only one condition previously required in those who desire admission into these Societies; viz. "a desire to flee from the wrath to come, to be saved from their sins." But wherever this is really fixed in the soul it will be shown by its fruits. It is therefore expected of all who continue therein, that they should continue to evidence their desire of salvation,

First, By doing no harm, by avoiding evil in every kind; especially that which is most generally practised. Such is

The taking the name of God in vain;

The profaning the day of the Lord, either by doing ordinary work thereon, or by buying or selling;

Drunkenness; buying or selling spirituous liquors, or drinking them, unless in cases of extreme necessity;

Fighting, quarrelling, brawling; brother going to law with brother; returning evil for evil, or railing for railing; the using many words in buying or selling;

The buying or selling uncustomed goods;

The giving or taking things on usury; i.e. unlawful interest;

Uncharitable or unprofitable conversation; particularly speaking evil of magistrates or of ministers;

Doing to others as we would not they should do unto us;

Doing what we know is not for the glory of God; as

The putting on of gold or costly apparel;

The taking such diversions as cannot be used in the name of the Lord Jesus;

The singing those songs, or reading those books which do not tend to the knowledge or love of God;

Softness, and needless self-indulgence;

Laying up treasures upon earth;

Borrowing without a probability of paying; or taking up goods without a probability of paying for them.

5. It is expected of all who continue in these Societies, that they should continue to evidence their desire of salvation,

Secondly, By doing good, by being in every kind merciful after their power; as they have opportunity, doing good of every possible sort, and as far as is possible, to all men;

To their bodies, of the ability that God giveth, by giving food to the hungry, by clothing the naked, by visiting or helping them that are sick or in prison;

To their souls, by instructing, reproving, or exhorting all they have any intercourse with; trampling under foot that enthusiastic doctrine of devils; that "we are not to do good, unless our heart be free to it."

By doing good especially to them that are of the household of faith, or groaning so to be; employing them preferably to others, buying one of another, helping each other in business; and so much the more, because the world will love its own, and them only.

By all possible diligence and frugality, that the gospel be not blamed.

By running with patience the race that is set before them, denying themselves, and taking up their cross daily; submitting to bear the reproach of Christ; to be as the filth and offscouring of the world; and looking that men should say all manner of evil of them falsely, for the Lord's sake.

6. It is expected of all who desire to continue in these Societies, that they should continue to evidence their desire of salvation,

Thirdly, By attending upon all the ordinances of God; such are,

The public worship of God;

The ministry of the word, either read or expounded;

The Supper of the Lord;

Family and private prayer;

Searching the Scriptures; and

Fasting or abstinence.

7. These are the General Rules of our Societies: all which we are taught of God to observe, even in His written word, the only rule, and the sufficient rule, both of our faith and practice. And all these we know His Spirit writes on every truly awakened heart. If there be any among us who observe them not, who habitually break any of them, let it be made known unto them who watch over that soul, as they that must give an account. We will admonish him of the error of his ways: we will bear with him for a season. But then if he repent not, he hath no more place among us. We have delivered our own souls.

Rules of the Bands
1744
(Wesleyan)

The design of our meeting is to obey that command of God, "Confess your faults one to another, and pray for one another that ye may be healed" (James 5:16).

To this end, we intend:

1. To meet once a week, at the least.

2. To come punctually at the hour appointed, without some extraordinary reason.

3. To begin (those of us who are present) exactly at the hour, with singing or prayer.

4. To speak each of us in order, freely and plainly, the true state of our souls, with the faults we have committed in thought, word, or deed, and the temptations we have felt since our last meeting.

5. To end every meeting with prayer suited to the state of each person present.

6. To desire some person among us to speak his own state first, and then to ask the rest, in order, as many and as searching questions as may be, concerning their state, sins, and temptations.

Endnotes

Introduction

[1] For further clarification of "cell church" and "house church" the reader is referred to the Resources page and the recommended reading there (page 111).

[2] Hare et al. 1994:1

Chapter 1

[1] Avis 1983:109 from *Luther's Works* (henceforth LW). Fortress Press and Concordia: Philadelphia and St. Louis. 1955. 36:88

[2] Zersen 1981:235

[3] Zersen 1981:235 from LW 13:111

[4] Further details on these points are available in Zersen 1981.

[5] Extract from the *Preface to the German Mass and Order of Divine Service*. Jan. 1526, available in B.J. Kidd (ed). 1911:193-202

[6] in Littel 1964:77

[7] to be found in Harder 1985:204

[8] in Littell 1964:130

[9] for example Bellardi 1934

[10] See, for example, the title of Beckham's *The Second Reformation* (Beckham 1995)

[11] in Hammann 1994:138.

[12] in Hammann 1994:142 (my translation)

Chapter 2

[1] in Tiller 1982:10

[2] in Hambrick-Stowe 1994:18

[3] Baxter 1656:10 in Green 1970:219

[4] in Ward 1992:281-2

Chapter 3

[1] Weborg C. J. "Pietism: The Fire of God which...Flames in the heart of Germany" in *Covenant Quarterly* 43 1985:14 quoted in Derksen 1986:18

[2] Enger, Trond. "Pietism" in *Westminster Dictionary of Christian Spirituality.* Gordon S. Wakefield (ed). Philadelphia: The Westminster Press. 1983:301 in Derksen1986:19

[3] Paragraph 61, Minutes of General Synod of Cleve, 1674 in Stoeffler 1973:219 taken from E Dresbach *Pragmatische Kirchengeschichte der preussischen Provinzen Rheinland und Westfalen* 1931:587-8

Chapter 4

[1] *Philipp Jakob Speners deutsche und lateinische theologische Bedenken*, 1838 edition: 435 in Stoeffler 1971:235

[2] Letter to the Philo-Biblical College at Leipzig in Brown 1978:80

[3] From "Of the Christian Church" (preached 1687) in Snyder1989:90

[4] From Snyder 1989:91

[5] Spener. *The Spiritual Priesthood.* 1677. Text in Erb 1983:50

6 Spener. *Erbauliche Evangelische—und Epistolische Sonntags—Andachten* Frankfurt, 1716:638 in Tappert 1964:13

7 Spener's account in *Consilia et Iudicia theological latina* Halle. 1709

8 Spener. *Sendschreiben* 51 in Wallmann 1986:295 (my translation)

9 *Pia Desideria* (Spener 1964:91)

10 *Spiritual Priesthood* section 63, (Erb 1983:63). (Spener's italics).

11 Spener. *Pia Desideria* 1964:89-90

12 Spener. *Erzehlung vom Pietismo* in Snyder 1989:107

13 in Gillies1981:237

Chapter 5
1 Alexander Mack quoted in Donald F Durnbaugh (ed). *European Origins of the Brethren* (Elgin, Ill. Brethren Press 1958:73) in Durnbaugh. 1985:121

Chapter 6
1 by Josiah Woodward. Extracts are to be found in Gillies 1981:258-271.

2 ibid:260

3 ibid:260

4 Gillies 1981:261

5 A full list of the rules is to be found in Kidder 1698:13-16.

6 Horneck. *The Sirenes; or, Delight and Judgment* (London 1690) in Duffy 1977:290

7 It is interesting, however, to note that both Cave and Horneck subsequently changed their view that it was possible or even desirable to return to New Testament church. It is likely that broader political events, particularly the trauma of the ousting of the king in 1688, caused them to become concerned and disillusioned that such attempts were possible. See Duffy 1977

8 *A Summary Account* 1697:25-26

9 Koch 1998: 90

10 Woodward 1698:69-71 from Hunsicker1996:195 and Gillies 1981:265

11 These quotations from the *Account* can be found in Gillies 1981:255-256

Chapter 7
1 in Daniel-Rops 1963:100

2 John Wesley 1741:13

Chapter 8
1 quoted in Van der Linde 1957:422

2 Zinzendorf 1973: 25-26

3 Zinzendorf. *Twenty-one Discourses or Dissertations upon the Augsburg Confession, Which is also the Brethren's Confession of Faith: Deliver'd by the Ordinary of the Brethren's Churches before the Seminary.* trans F Okeley, London: Bowyer. 1753:243-44 in Snyder 1989:149

4 *Herrnhut Diary* 19 December 1732 in Frör 1974:87 (my translation)

5 Spangenberg. *Leben des Herrn Nicolas Ludwig Grafen und Herrn von Zinzendorf und Pottendorf.* 1772-75:432 in Frör 1974:84 (my translation).

6 Zinzendorf *Rede vom Grund-Pläne unserer Heidenmissionen* in Bintz 1979:99 (my translation).

Endnotes

[7]   *Herrnhuter Diarium* 15 January 1735 in Frör 1974:92 (my translation).
[8]   Weinlick 1956:85
[9]   see Ward 1992:143 for further details.

Chapter 9
[1]   letter from J. Clayton to John Wesley, 4 Sept.1732 in Wesley, *Journal* 8:281
[2]   *Journals and Diaries* 18:476 in Heitzenrater 1995:66
[3]   *Journal* I:226-230 (10 June 1736)
[4]   Henderson 1997:121 quoting Charles Goodell, *The Drillmaster of Methodism* New York: Eaton and Mains, 1902:239
[5]   *Works* VIII:125-6 in Hunsicker 1996:209
[6]   in Heitzenrater 1995:27-28
[7]   *Works* 13:55 in Snyder 1989:201
[8]   quoted in Henderson 1997:167
[9]   E P Thompson. *The Making of the English Working Class*. London 1963 quoted in Hempton. 1983:20
[10] Smith 1988, for example, analyses the composition of the Keighly Circuit in 1763 and finds the 1,198 members included 3 gentlemen, 10 professionals, 135 in agriculture, 21 in commerce, 164 in the trades and crafts, 270 weavers, 406 spinners. This was not a group of idle poor or the flotsam and jetsam of society.

Chapter 10
[1]   Wesley. *Works* 3:445 in Snyder 1996:43.
[2]   Duling 1995
[3]   Gillies 1981:260
[4]   Quoted in Van der Linde 1957:422
[5]   Gillies 1981:256
[6]   *Journal*, 24 May 1738
[7]   For further details on this see Duling 1995, Esler 1987, 1995, Kloppenborg 1996, McCready 1996, S.G. Wilson 1996.
[8]   *Spiritual Priesthood*, section 63 (Erb 1983:63)

Chapter 11
[1]   Hare et al 1994:82
[2]   Davies J. 1984:47. Davies quotes the psychotherapist Carl Rogers: "to be optimally effective the group must be relevant to the organization, family, and life environment of the person" from Carl Rogers on *Encounter Groups* New York: Harper and Row 1973:130.
[3]   Snyder 1989 deals in depth with the issue of different types of renewal movements and Bunton 1998 examines the role of cell groups in these renewal movements.
[4]   Malina 1986:14
[5]   Troeltsch E. *The Social Teaching of the Christian Churches* 2 vols. New York: Harper & Brothers—translation of *Die Soziallehren der christlichen Kirchen und Gruppen, Gesammelte Schriften I*, Tubingen: Mohr (Siebeck). 1912. 2nd edition 1919
[6]   Hare et al 1994:186. This is based on D. V. Fisher, "A Conceptual Analysis of Self-disclosure" in *Journal for the Theory of Social Behaviour*. 14: 277-96
[7]   Hare et al 1994—chapter one.

Bibliography

Anon. *A Summary Account of the Life of the truly pious and reverend Dr. Anthony Horneck, Minster of the Savoy, in a Letter to Friend.* London: E. Whitlock. 1697

Arndt, Johann. *True Christianity* (trans. P Erb). London: SPCK. 1979

Astin, Howard. *Body and Cell—Making the Transition to Cell Church—A First-hand Account.* Crowborough: Monarch, 1998

Avis, P. "Luther's Theology of the Church" in *The Churchman* 97:2, 1983. 104-11

Bainton, Roland H. *Here I Stand: A Life of Martin Luther.* Nashville: Abingdon Press. 1950

Banks, R. *Paul's Idea of Community—The Early House Churches in their Historical Setting.* Exeter: Paternoster Press. 1980

Banks, R. & Banks, J. *The Church Comes Home—A New Base for Community and Mission.* Oxford: Albatross Books/Lion Publishing. 1989

Baudert, S. "Zinzendorf's thought on Missions related to his views of the World" in *International Review of Missions* XXI:83 (July 1932). 390-401

Beckham, William A. *The Second Reformation—Reshaping the Church for the 21st Century.* Houston: Touch Publications. 1995

Bellardi, Werner. *Geschichte der "Christlichen Gemeinschaften" in Strassburg (1546-1550).* Leipzig: M.Heinsius Nachfolger. 1934

Bessières, R.P. *Au temps de Saint Vincent de Paul—Deuxgrands méconnus— précurseurs de l'action Catholique et sociale: Gaston de Renty et Henry Buch.* Paris: Aux Editions Spes. 1931

Bintz (ed). *Texte zur Mission.* Hamburg: Wittig Verlag. 1979

Blasi, Anthony J. "Role Structures in the Early Hellenistic Church" in *Sociological Analysis* 47:3 (1986). 226-48

Bloesch, Donald G.. *The Evangelical Renaissance.* London: Hodder & Stoughton. 1974

Brown, Dale W. *Understanding Pietism,* Grand Rapids: Eerdmans. 1978 "The Wesleyan Revival from a Pietist Perspective" in *Wesleyan Theological Journal* 24 (1989). 7-17

Bullock, F.W.B. *Voluntary Religious Societies 1520-1799.* St. Leonard's-on-Sea: Budd & Gillatt. 1963

Bunton, Peter. *Cell Groups in Protestant Church History: An Investigation into the Use of Small Groups in the Seventeenth and Eighteenth Centuries with Implications for the Church's Life and Mission today.* Unpublished M.A. Dissertation. All Nations Christian College, Hertfordshire, England. 1998

Cahill, Thomas. *How the Irish Saved Civilization: The Untold Story of Ireland's Heroic Role from the Fall of Rome to the Rise of Medieval Europe,* London: Hodder & Stoughton. 1995

Chadwick, Henry. *The Early Church,* Middlesex: Penguin. 1967

Collins, Kenneth J. "John Wesley's Critical Appropriation of Early German Pietism" in *Wesleyan Theological Journal* 27 (Spr-Fall 1992). 57-92

Conn, Harvie. "Small Groups and Renewal: A Ghana Case Study" in *City Watch* 9:1 (First Quarter 1994). 4

Cross, F.L. & Livingstone, E.A.(eds). *The Oxford Dictionary of the Christian Church.* Oxford: O.U.P. 1997

Currie, R., Gilbert, A. and Horsely, L. *Churches and Churchgoers: Patterns of Church Growth in the British Isles Since 1700.* Oxford: Clarendon. 1977

Daniel-Rops, H. *The Church in the Seventeenth Century.* London: J.M. Dent. 1963

Danker, William J. *Profit for the Lord—Economic Activities in Moravian Missions and the Basel Mission Trading Company.* Grand Rapids: Eerdmans. 1971

Davies, A. *The Moravian Revival of 1727 and Some of its Consequences.* The Evangelical Library—Annual Lecture.

Davies, J. "Small groups; are they really so new?" in *Christian Education Journal* 5:2 (1984). 43-52

Davies, R.E. *The Contribution to Mission Principles of the Moravian Church, the Renewed Unity of Brethren, as seen particularly in it Origins.* Unpublished paper from Fuller SWM. March 1988

Lay Leadership in the Eighteenth Century Awakening. Unpublished paper from Fuller SWM. 1988

Davies, Wilma G. *A Ticket to heaven? A Sociological Study of the Tien Tao in Relation to Their Understandings of "Salvation."* Unpublished MA dissertation: All Nations Christian College. 1994

Derksen, Kenneth J. *"The Collegium Pietatis* as a model for modern home Bible study groups" in Crux 22: 4 (D1986). 16-25.

Doraisamy, Theodore R. *What God Hath Wrought: Motives of Mission in Methodism from Wesley to Thoburn.* Singapore: Methodist Book Room. 1983

Dorner, J.A. *History of Protestant Theology—Particularly in Germany.* Edinburgh: T & T Clark. 1871

Douglas, Mary. *Natural Symbols—Explorations in Cosmology.* London: Routledge. 1996 (first pub 1970)

Duffy, E. "Primitive Christianity Revived: Religious Renewal in Augustan England" in Baker, Derek (ed) *Renaissance and Renewal in Christian History.* Oxford: Basil Blackwell. 1977. 287-300

Duling, Dennis, C. "Social-Scientific Small Group Research and Second Testament Study" in *Biblical Theology Bulletin* 25 (Winter 1995). 179-193

Durnbaugh, Donald, F. *The Believers' Church—the History and Character of Radical Protestantism.* Scottsdale, PA: Herald Press. 1985

Elliott, John H. "The Jewish Messianic Movement—From Faction to Sect" in *Modelling Early Christianity—Social-scientific Studies of the New Testament in its Context,* Philip F. Esler (ed). London and New York: Routledge. 1995. 96-113

Erb, Peter, C. *Pietists: Selected Writings.* London: SPCK. 1983

Esler, Philip F. (ed). *Community and Gospel in Luke-Acts: The Social and Political Motivations of Lucan Theology.* Cambridge: CUP. 1987

Modelling Early Christianity: Social-scientific Studies of the New Testament in Its Context. London and New York: Routledge. 1995

Freeman, A. J. *The Hermeneutics of Count Ludwig von Zinzendorf.* Unpublished Ph.D. Dissertation, Princeton Theological Seminary. 1962

Fries, Adelaide, L. *Customs and Practices of the Moravian Church.* Winston-Salem, NC: Moravian Church. 1973

Frör, Peter. "Gruppenseelsorge in der kirchlichen Tradition: das Beispiel der Banden Herrnhuts" in *Perspektiven der Pastoralpsychologie.* R. Riess (ed). Göttingen: Vandenhoeck & Ruprecht. 1974. 79-95.

Garrison, David. *Church Planting Movements.* Richmond, VA: International Mission Board—Southern Baptist Convention. 1999

Gaustad, Edwin S. "Quest for Pure Christianity" in Christian History Vol XIII, No.1 1994. 8-13

Gillies, John. *Historical Collections of Accounts of Revival.* Fairfield, PA: Banner of Truth. 1981 (originally 1754)

Green, Michael. *Evangelism in the Early Church.* London: Hodder & Stoughton. 1970

Greshat, Martin. "The Relation between Church and Civil Community in Bucer's Reforming Work" in Wright, D.F.(ed). *Martin Bucer: Reforming Church and Community.* Cambridge: C.U.P. 1994. 17-31.

Hambrick-Stowe, Charles, E. "Ordering their Private World—What Puritans Did to Grow Spiritually" in *Christian History* Vol. XIII, No 1, 1994. 16-19.

Hamilton, J. Taylor and Hamilton, Kenneth, G. *The History of the Moravian Church: The Renewed Unitas Fratrum 1722-1957.* Bethlehem, PA: Moravian Church in America. 1967

Hamilton, Kenneth G.. *A History of the Missions of the Moravian Church During the Eighteenth and Nineteenth Centuries.* Bethlehem, PA: Times Publishing Company. 1901

"Cultural Contributions of Moravian Missions among the Indians" in *Pennsylvania History* XVIII No.1 (Jan 1954)

Hamilton, Malcolm B. *The Sociology of Religion—Theoretical and Comparative Perspectives.* London/New York: Routledge. 1995

Hammann, Gottfried. *Entre le secte et la cité: Le projet d'Eglise de réformateur Martin Bucer* (1491-1551). Geneva: Labor et Fides. 1984

"Ecclesiological motifs behind the creation of the 'Christlichen Gemeinschaften'" in Wright, D.F.(ed), *Martin Bucer: Reforming Church and Community.* Cambridge: C.U.P. 1994. 129-143

Hanby, Mark. *You Have Not Many Fathers.* Shippensburg, PA: Destiny Image Publishers. 1996

Harder, Leland (ed). *Sources of Swiss Anabaptism.* Scottsdale, PA: Herald Press. 1985

Hare, A. Paul (et al). *Small Group Research: A Handbook.* Norwood, NJ: Ablex Publishing Corporation. 1994

Harper, George W. "New England Dynasty—The Lives and Legacies of the Mathers, America's Most Influential Puritan Family" in *Christian History* Vol. XIII, No 1 (1994). 20-22

Heidenbrecht, Paul. "Learning from Nature: The Educational Legacy of Jan Amos Comenius" in *Christian History* Vol.VI:1 (1987). 22-3,35

Heitzenrater, Richard P. *Wesley and the People called Methodists.* Nashville: Abingdon Press. 1995

Hempton, P. "Evangelical revival and society: a historiographical review of Methodism and British Society c1750-1850" in *Themelios* 8:3 (April 1983). 19-25

Henderson, D. Michael. *John Wesley's Class Meeting—A Model for Making Disciples.* Nappanee, IN: Evangel Publishing House. 1997

Hunsicker, David S. "John Wesley: Father of Today's Small Group Concept?" in *Wesleyan Theological Journal* 31 (spring 1996). 192-211

Irwin, Joyce. "Anna Maria van Schurman and Antoinette Bourignon: Contrasting Examples of Seventeenth-Century Pietism" in *Church History* 60:3 (Sept 1991). 301-315

Jedin, Hubert & Delan, John (eds). *History of the Church.* Vol. VI. London: Burns & Oates. 1981

Joubert, Stephan J. "Managing the Household—Paul as *paterfamilias* of the Christian Household Group in Corinth" in Philip Esler (ed). *Modelling Early Christianity—Social-scientific Studies of the New Testament in its Context.* London and New York: Routledge. 1995. 213-223

Kidd, B.J.(ed). *Documents Illustrative of the Continental Reformation,* Oxford: Clarendon Press. 1911

Kidder, Richard. *The Life of the Reverend Anthony Horneck, D.D. Late Preacher at the Savoy.* London: J.H. & B. Aylmer. 1698

Kittelson, James. "Martin Bucer and the Ministry of the Church" in Wright, D.F.(ed). *Martin Bucer: Reforming Church and Community.* Cambridge: C.U.P. 1994. 83-94

Klaassen, Walter. "A Fire that Spread—Anabaptist Beginnings" in *Christian History.* Vol. IV. No1 (1985). 7-9

Kloppenborg, John S. "Collegia and Thiasoi: Issues in Function, Taxonomy and Membership" in *Voluntary Associations in the Graeco-Roman World,* John S. Kloppenborg & Stephen G. Wilson (eds). London/New York: Routledge. 1996. 16-30

Koch, George B (ed). *The Country Parson's Advice to his Parishioners.* London: Monarch. 1998 (Originally published 1680).

Krallmann, Günter. *Mentoring for Mission—A Handbook on Leadership Principles Exemplified by Jesus Christ.* Hong Kong: Jensco. 1992

Kreider, Larry. *House to House: Spiritual Insights for the 21st Century Church.* Pennsylvania: House to House Publications. 1995

Lewis, A. "Ecclesia ex auditu: a Reformed view of the Church as the community of the Word of God" in *Scottish Journal of Theology* 35:1 (1982). 13-32

Lewis, A.J. *Zinzendorf the Ecumenical Pioneer: A Study of the Moravian Contribution to Christian Mission and Unity.* London: SCM. 1962

Lim, Isaac. "Wesleyan preaching and the small group ministry: principles and practices" in *Asia Journal of Theology* 3:2 (O 1989). 509-523

Littell, Franklin H. *The Origins of Sectarian Protestantism.* New York: Macmillan.1964

Malina, Bruce J. *Christian Origins and Cultural Anthropology—Practical Models for Biblical Interpretation.* Atlanta: John Knox Press. 1986

"Early Christian Groups—Using Small Group Formation Theory to Explain Christian Organizations" in Esler Philip (ed). *Modelling Early Christianity—Social-scientific Studies of the New Testament in its Context.* London and New York: Routledge. 1995. 96-113

Marins, Jose. "Basic ecclesial communities in Latin America" in *International Review of Mission* 68 (July 1979). 235-242

McCready, Wayne O. *"Ekklesia* and Voluntary Associations" in *Voluntary Associations in the Graeco-Roman World.* John S. Kloppenborg & Stephen G. Wilson (eds). London/New York: Routledge. 1996. 59-73

Mellis, Charles J. *Committed Communities—Fresh Streams for World Missions.* Pasadena: William Carey Library. 1976

Neighbour, Ralph, W. *Where Do We Go From Here? A Guidebook for the Cell Group Church.* Touch Publications: Houston. 1990

Noll, Mark, A. "Martin Luther and the concept of a true church" in *The Evangelical Quarterly* 50:2 (Apr-Jun 1978). 79-85

Pauck, W. *Melanchthon and Bucer.* Library of Christian Classics XIX. London: S.C.M. Press. 1969

Pelikan, J. *Spirit versus Structure—Luther and the Institutions of the Church.* London: Collins. 1968

Peter, Rodolphe. "Informal Groups in the Reformation: Rhenish Types" in *Informal Groups in the Church.* R Metz & J Schlick (eds). Pittsburgh: Pickwick. 1975. 214-231

Pointer, Roy. *How do Churches Grow?* Basingstoke: Marshall, Morgan & Scott. 1984

Prozesky, Martin H. "The Emergence of Dutch Pietism" in *Journal of Ecclesiastical History* 28:1 (Jan 1977). 29-38

Rack, Henry, D. *Reasonable Enthusiast: John Wesley and the Rise of Methodism.* London: Epworth Press. 1992

"Domestic visitation—Nineteenth century evangelism" in *Journal of Ecclesiastical History* 24:4 (Oct 1973). 357-376

Rapp, Francis. "Informal Groups at the End of the Middle Ages: Rhenish Types" in *Informal Groups in the Church.* R. Metz and J Schlick (eds). Pittsburgh:The Pickwick Press. 1975. 197-213

Runia, Klaas. "Evangelicals and the doctrine of the church in European church history" in *Evangelical Review of Theology* 8 (Apr 1984). 40-57

Sattler, Gary. "Moving on Many Fronts" in *Christian History* Vol. V: No2 (1986). 20-22

Schattschneider, D.A. "Souls for the Lamb": *A Theology for the Christian Mission According to Count Nicolaus Ludwig Von Zinzendorf and Bishop*

Augustus Gottlieb Spangenberg. University of Chicago. unpublished Ph.D. dissertation. 1975

"Pioneers in Mission: Zinzendorf and the Moravians" in *International Bulletin of Missionary Research* 8:2 (Apr 1984). 63-67

Schwarz, Christian A. *Natural Church Development—a Guide to Eight Essential Qualities of Healthy Churches.* Carol Stream, IL: ChurchSmart Resources. 1996

Seguy, Jean. "The Internal Dynamics of Informal Groups" in *Informal Groups in the Church.* R. Metz and J. Schlick (eds). Pittsburgh: Pickwick Press. 1975. 35-70

Simson, Wolfgang. *Houses That Change the World.* Carlisle: OM Publishing. 2001

Skevington Wood, A. "The Priesthood of all believers" in *Christian Graduate* June 1964. 8-11

"The Eighteenth Century Methodist Revival Reconsidered" in *The Evangelical Quarterly* 53:3 (July-Sept 1981). 130-148

Smaby, Beverly Prior. *The Transformation of Moravian Bethlehem: From Communal Mission to Family Economy.* Philadelphia: University of Pennsylvania Press. 1988

Smith, J. Q. "Occupational groups among the early Methodists of the Keighly Circuit" in *Church History* 57:2 (June 1988). 187-196

Snyder, Howard A. *The Community of the King.* Downers Grove: IVP. 1978

The Radical Wesley—and Patterns for Church Renewal. Downers Grove: IVP. 1980

Liberating the Church—the Ecology of Church and Kingdom. Basingstoke: Marshall Paperbacks. 1983

Signs of the Spirit—How God Reshapes the Church. Grand Rapids: Academie Books/Zondervan. 1989

Radical Renewal: The Problem of Wineskins Today. Houston: Touch Publications. 1996

Sommer, Elisabeth. "A Different Kind of Freedom? Order and Discipline among the Moravian Brethren in Germany and Salem, North Carolina 1771-1801" in *Church History* 63 (June 1994). 221-234

Spangenberg, Augustus, G. *An Account of the Manner in Which the Protestant Church of the Unitas Fratrum, or United Brethren, Preach the Gospel, and Carry on Their Missions among the Heathen.* London: Brethren's Society for the Furtherance of the Gospel. 1788

Spehn, Mel, R. "Small-group religion" in *Pastoral Psychology* 23 (Jan 1972). 50-58

Spener, Phillip Jakob. *Pia Desideria.* 1675. Theodore G Tappert, trans. Philadelphia: Fortress Press. 1964

Letzte Theologische Bedenken. Hesse: Wäusenhaus. 1711

Stampe, L. K. *The Moravian Missions at the Time of Zinzendorf—Principles and Methods.* Unpublished M Sacred Theology Dissertation. Union Theological Seminary. 1947

Stark, R. "How New Religions Succeed—A Theoretical Model" in D. G. Bromley and P. E. Hammond (eds). *The Future of New Religious Movements.* Macon: Mercer University Press. 1987. 11-30

Steele, Richard B. "John Wesley's Synthesis of the Revival Practices of Jonathan Edwards, George Whitefield, Nicholas von Zinzendorf" in *Wesleyan Theological Journal* 30 (Spring 1995). 154-172

Stephens, W.P. *The Holy Spirit in the Theology of Martin Bucer.* Cambridge: C.U.P. 1970

Stoeffler, F. Ernest. *The Rise of Evangelical Pietism.* Leiden: E.J.Brill. 1971

German Pietism During the Eighteenth Century. Leiden: E.J.Brill. 1973

"Can These Bones Live?" in *Christian History* Vol. V: No2 (1986). 9-12

Stupperich, R. (ed.). *Martin Bucer: Deutsche Schriften.* Gütersloh. 1960

Tappert, Theodore G. *Pia Desideria* by Philip Jacob Spener. Translated, edited with introduction. Philadelphia: Fortress Press. 1964

Thompson, H.P. *Into All Lands: The History of the Society for the Propagation of the Gospel in Foreign Parts* 1701-1950. London: SPCK. 1951

Tiller, John. *Puritan, Pietist and Pentecostalist: Three types of Evangelical Spirituality.* Bramcote, Notts: Grove Books. 1982

Van der Linde, J. "Community and Mission: The Moravian Model" in *Evangelical Review of Theology* 2:1 (April 1978). 89-102

"The Moravian Church in the World 1457-1957" in *International Review of Mission* XLVI:No 184 (Oct 1957). 417-423

Walker, Andrew. *Restoring the Kingdom.* Guildford: Eagle. 1998

Walker-Ramisch, Sandra. "Graeco-Roman Voluntary Associations and The Damascus Document: A Sociological Analysis" in *Voluntary Associations in the Graeco-Roman World.* John S. Kloppenborg & Stephen G. Wilson (eds). London and New York: Routledge. 1996. 128-145

Wallace, Anthony, F.C. *Religion—An Anthropological View.* New York: Random House. 1966

Wallmann, Johannes. *Philipp Jakob Spener und die Anfänge des Pietismus.* Tübingen: J.C.B. Mohr (Paul Siebeck). 1986

Walsh, Michael. *Roots of Christianity.* London: Griffen Books. 1986

Ward, W. R. "The renewed Unity of the Brethren " in *Bulletin of the John Rylands Library of the University of Manchester* 70 (1988). 77-92

The Protestant Evangelical Awakening. Cambridge: CUP. 1992

"German Pietism, 1670-1750—A Bibliographical Survey" in *Journal of Ecclesiastical History* Vol. 44: No 3 (July 1993). 476-505

"Pastoral Office and the General Priesthood in the Great Awakening" in *Faith and Faction.* W.R. Ward (ed). London: Epworth Press. 1993. 177-201

Weborg, John, C. "Reborn in order to Renew" in *Christian History* Vol. V, No2, (1986). 17-18,34-35

Weinlick, John R. *Count Zinzendorf—The Story of his Life and Leadership in The Renewed Moravian Church.* Nashville: Abingdon Press. 1956

Wesley, John. *An Extract of the life of Monsieur de Renty—A late Nobleman of France.* London: Strahan. 1741

The Journal of John Wesley M.A., Sometime Fellow of Lincoln College, Oxford, Nehemiah Curnock (ed). London: Charles H. Kelley 1909. Vols., I, II and VIII

Works London: Wesleyan Conference Office. 1881. Vols. VIII and XIII

White, L. Michael. "Sociological Analysis of Early Christian Groups: A Social Historian's Response" in *Sociological Analysis* 47:3 (1986). 249-66

Williams, George H. "'Congregationalist' Luther and the Free Churches" in *Lutheran Quarterly*, XIX (August 1967). 283-295

Wilson, Bryan (ed). *Patterns of Sectarianism: Organization and Ideology in Social and Religious Movements.* London: Heinemann. 1967

Religious Sects. London: Weidenfeld and Nicolson. 1970

Religion in Sociological Perspective. Oxford: OUP. 1982

The Social Dimensions of Sectarianism—Sects and New Religious Movements in Contemporary Society. Oxford: Clarendon Press. 1990

"Persistence of Sects" in *Indian Missiological Review* 17:2 (June 1995). 20-32

Wilson, Stephen G. "Voluntary Associations: An Overview" in *Voluntary Associations in the Graeco-Roman World.* John S. Kloppenborg & Stephen G. Wilson (eds). London and New York: Routledge. 1996. 1-15

Winter, Ralph D. "The Two Structures of God's Redemptive Mission" in *Missiology* 2:1 Autumn (January 1974). 121-39

Wright, D.F. (ed). *Martin Bucer: Reforming Church and Community,* Cambridge: C.U.P. 1994

Zersen, David. "Lutheran roots for small group ministry" in *Currents in Theology and Mission* 8 (Aug 1981). 234-238

Zinzendorf, N.L. *Nine Public Lectures on Important Subjects in Religion Preached in Fetter Lane Chapel in London in the Year 1746.* George Forell (translator and editor). Iowa City: University of Iowa Press. 1973

Cell Group and House Church
Resources

Church Planting Movements, David Garrison

Groups of Twelve, Joel Comiskey

Helping You Build Cell Churches, Compiled by Brian Sauder and Larry Kreider

House Church Networks: A Church For a New Generation, Larry Kreider

House to House, Larry Kreider

Loving the Lost—The Principles and Practice of Cell Church, Laurence Singlehurst

Where Do We Go From Here? Ralph Neighbour

Web site of Cell UK: www.cellchurch.co.uk

Web site of DOVE Christian Fellowship International and House to House Publications: www.dcfi.org

Cell-based Ministry Seminars

• Cell Group Ministry Seminar
• Spiritual Fathering and Mothering Seminar
• Youth Cell Ministry Seminar
• Counseling Basics for Small Group Leaders
• Cell-based Church Planting Clinic
• Fivefold Ministry Seminar
• Evangelism Seminar
• Pre- and Postmarriage Mentor's Training Seminar
Held at various locations throughout the US and Canada

Cell-based Audio Materials

• Cell Groups
• Leadership Training For Elders
• Planting the Cell Church
• Spiritual Fathering and Mothering
• Youth Cells and Youth Ministry
• many others

Cell-based Resources

• *House To House*
• *Helping You Build Cell Churches Manual*
• *The Cry for Spiritual Fathers and Mothers*
• Destination Cell Church
• many others

For more information about these seminars and cell-based resources
Web site: www.dcfi.org
Email: dcfi@dcfi.org
Call: 800-848-5892 USA